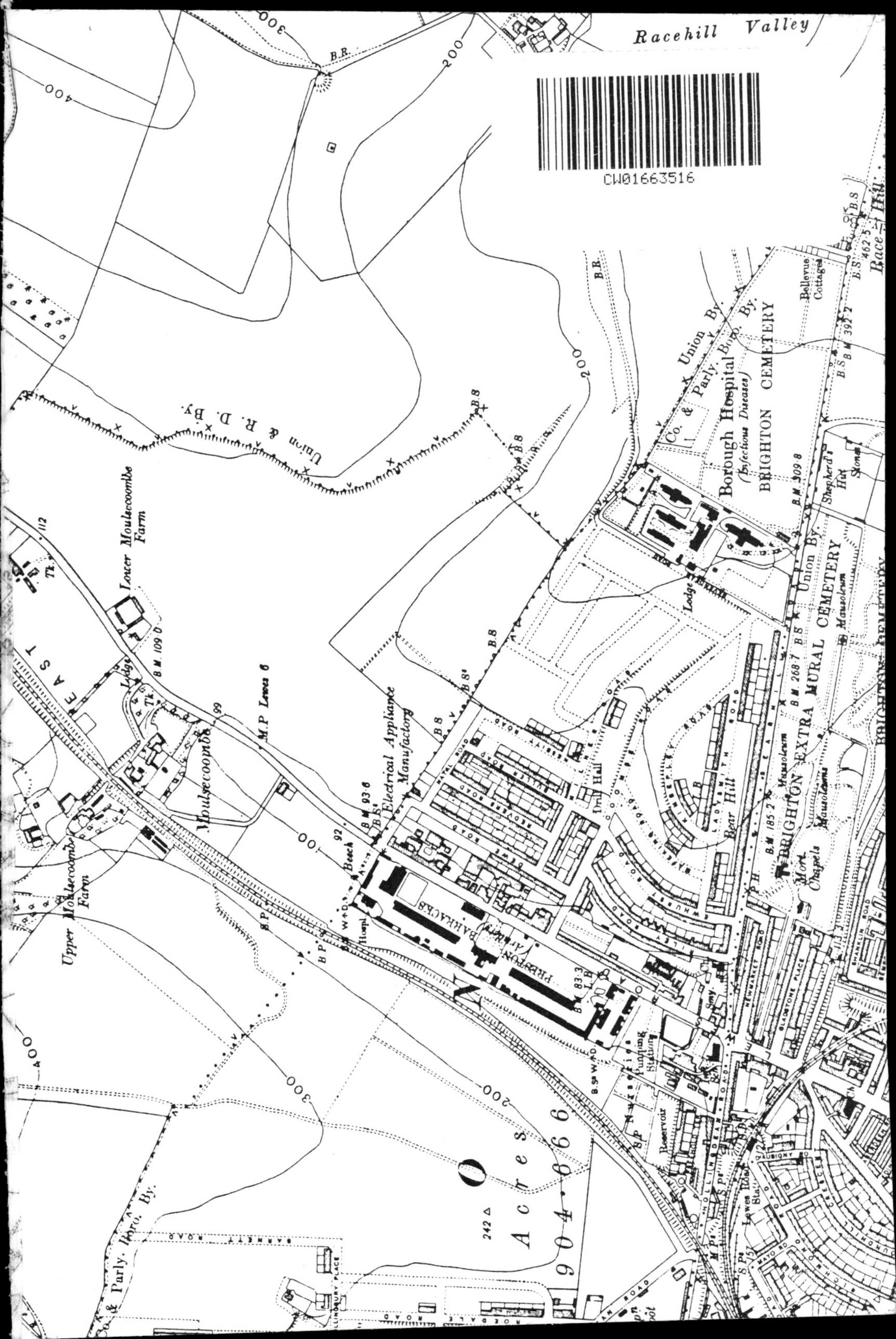

Racehill Valley
Race Hill
Bellevue Cottages
BRIGHTON CEMETERY
Borough Hospital (Infectious Diseases)
Co. & Parly. Boro. By.
Union By.
Union & R. D. By.
Lower Moulsecoombe Farm
Upper Moulsecoombe Farm
Moulsecoombe
Lodge
M.P. Lewes 6
Electrical Appliance Manufactory
Beech
Drill Hall
Bear Hill
BRIGHTON EXTRA MURAL CEMETERY
Mausoleum
Mort. Chapels
Shepherd's Hut
PRESTON Artillery BARRACKS
Pumping Station
Reservoir
Lewes Road Sta.
Acres 904·666
Co. & Parly. Boro. By.
EAST

Six-inch Ordnance Survey Maps

Inside front cover: 1912 map showing nothing but farms and open country beyond the old Preston Barracks.

Inside back cover: 1932 map showing the area before the building of East Moulsecoomb between 1936 and 1939.

Note the old spelling, Moulsecoombe, on some old maps and photos.

Ruby Dunn

MOULSECOOMB DAYS

Learning and Teaching on a Brighton Council Estate 1922-1947

QueenSpark Book 23

Chapter I

HOMES FIT FOR HEROES

My first acquaintance with Moulsecoomb was in 1922, when as an infant of 18 months, I was wheeled in my pram to number 8 The Avenue, which was then a newly built house among builder's rubble, at the entrance to a beautiful Downland valley. My family loved it there, in the heart of the countryside. It was not long before I was old enough to enjoy the delights of playing on the wide green facing our house, or walking with my big sisters up to the head of the valley, to pick the wild scabious and poppies, or to play hide-and-seek among the corn stooks. I remember sitting on our wooden garden gate, when very small, and watching the ploughman with his horse, working on the land where Upper Bevendean now stands. I remember in my pre-school years, pushing my doll in her pram round and round the grass paths in our front garden, when friendly Mr Vic Taylor, pushing his baby Sheila in her pram, looked over the gate saying, "Would you like to swop?"

How did my father, born of an old Brighton family, come to live so far from the centre of the town he loved?

John Pennifold (known as Jack) was born in 1874, the oldest son and second child of John and Mary Pennifold, above the bakery run by his father in Ditchling Road, on the corner of Princes Road. His wife Mary Arnold also belonged to a Brighton family, who lived in Ditchling Road. They were Baptists and attended a Chapel off West Street, which has since been demolished to make way for a car park. The later generations of Arnolds were connected with the Baptist Church adjoining the Astoria Cinema, where Stanley Arnold was the organist.

Jack had four brothers, Walter, Bert, Dick and Tom, and an older sister, Caroline Ruth, known as "Sis". They all grew up in Brighton, and after their father's death, moved with their mother to Park Crescent, where she worked as housekeeper to an old gentleman.

Jack's schooling was scanty and finished abruptly at the age of thirteen, on his father's death, when he started a seven-year apprenticeship and became a master printer. He and his brother Walter then decided to emigrate to Australia, and Tom moved to Canada. Sis married the son of a baker, Charles Ralph of Tunbridge Wells, while Bert, a coachbuilder by trade, ran a shop in Jubilee Street. After the First World War, with a gradual return to health, he went into partnership with Mr Nicholls, who later had a business in North Road and became a successful contractor and an Alderman. News of his mother's ill-health brought Jack home, but Walter stayed on as he was engaged to an Australian girl, and the brothers never saw each other again.

On his return to England, Jack decided to leave Brighton and seek printing work elsewhere.He met Emmeline Furlonger (known as Emmie) while working in Reading. Her family, having previously lived in the Surrey village of Woking, were running the Turners Arms in Reading. Emmie, as the eldest daughter in a family of eight children, had to help in the bar. As her sisters grew older she was able to obtain more congenial work in the office of the Printing Works. Here it was that she first saw the dark and handsome printer behind his machine. (Her original description of "*tall,* dark and handsome" had to be modified when she discovered that he used to stand on a box to do his work!) A shared interest in cycling, combined with her mother's renowned hospitality at the Turners Arms, meant that before long Emmie and Jack became engaged.

It was a long and interrupted engagement, because Jack had other plans. Following his mother's death and the acquiring of a small legacy, he decided to try his luck in New Zealand as a printer, and Emmie would join him when he had made his fortune. After Emmie had seen him off at Tilbury her mother was heard to remark: "That's the last you'll see of *that* young man, my girl!" However, while enjoying his experiences which he recorded in a diary still in our possession, he found New Zealanders had a strong prejudice against "homeys" starting up in business, so he returned, still a poor man, to marry Emmie, at Greyfriars Church, Reading, in August 1910. Jack was then thirty-six and Emmie twenty-five.

With a promise of work, but very little savings, they went to Brighton for their honeymoon, spent in the back bedroom of brother Bert's shop. Emmie recalls that she was quite entranced by the bright lights of the town and likened the place to fairyland. "I hope it will always be like fairyland to you, my dear", her gallant husband replied. Emmie maintained that it always was, until the First World War blew their life to pieces.

Because of his age, Jack had a late call-up for Army Service in 1916. The years following the War were a distressing time, and he had his share of problems to face. He returned to Civvy Street in 1919, to find a noisy and violent family billeted on his wife, and poor prospects of work in the town. After being forced to take his wife and two children to Reading temporarily, in order to find work, he finally secured a job with the Southern Publishing Company in Robert Street, Brighton in 1920, as a master printer.

I was born in the following February. Mum already had two daughters, Irene (10) and Kathleen (6), and needed room for her expanding family. Dad, in desperation, went to the Housing Department, to see if anything could be done about re-housing the unruly family upstairs. We were then living near Five Ways, in Stanmer Park Road. My parents were told that nothing could be done for them, since the father, although an ex-soldier, was out of work and had no references. They were then asked by the Housing Manager if they had heard anything about the new "Garden Suburb", which was being built out on the road to Lewes. Would

A home in the country

Mrs Pennifold with Ruby, aged two, a year after moving to Moulsecoomb

The Pennifolds in their suburban garden, 1929

L to R: Irene (18), Ruby (8), Kathleen (14), with Mum and Dad in the background

they perhaps consider renting one of those new houses themselves?

Dad thought it was worth investigating and Mum liked what she saw. The semi-detached houses were set in a valley, looking more like country cottages. Mum was a countrywoman at heart, having spent her childhood in a village. Dad thought the rent was very high, but there were three nice bedrooms, and a big garden, and lighting and cooking was by electricity, which was the very latest fashion. So Mum tried a little persuasion, offering to help with expenses by earning money at home, if he would agree to take them away from the terrible family upstairs. Their name was added to the waiting list, and they moved into 8 The Avenue in the summer of 1922.

Despite his initial hesitation, my Dad was always pleased and proud to be living in Moulsecoomb in those early days. He used to tell our visiting relatives of the advantages of our new environment, while Mum would show her modern electric cooker and shiny copper kettle. Dad was proud of his work on the garden, and it became his chief hobby. I remember the fruit bushes and trees, and the harvests of black, red, and white currants, the gooseberries, blackberries, loganberries and apples. The front garden was always ablaze with colour in the summer, and one year Dad won a prize in the Annual Gardeners Competition.

Life in South Moulsecoomb in the 1920s was still more rural than suburban. I was told at school, that the name of our Estate was derived from the name of the original owner of the land, and was once Mull's Coomb or Valley. Where our houses stood, there had once been a pig farm, and everything Dad planted grew well. Moulsecoomb Place, the old Manor House, part Elizabethan with a Georgian front, stood back off the Lewes Road, at the entrance to our valley whose slopes were covered in cornfields. Sheep grazed at the head of the valley where the land rose towards Bevendean Farm.

On weekdays we were sent to play up the valley. At weekends we walked further afield with our parents, to search for bee-orchids behind Bates Farm, or to walk in Stanmer Park where we were permitted only to keep to the track. In spite of this restriction, my Dad knew where primroses, white violets and bluebells could be found in the Spring. We also footed it up Coldean Lane past West's Farm, to fish for tiddlers in the pond where the Community Hall now stands. Walking to Falmer Pond and dipping for tadpoles and newts was about the extent of our travels. It was not until I was about eight or nine that I was allowed to walk to Lewes with my big sister and go pond-dipping at Southover.

All the land on the west side of Lewes Road, between Moulsecoomb Place and Coldean Lane, was given over to fruit farms and nurseries, some of which belonged to Mr Bates and some to Mr Woollard. I remember the time when I was told that I was old enough to be allowed to cross Lewes Road on my own and walk to Bates Nursery to buy the fruit for our family; the scent of the stored fruit as I entered the wooden sheds, and watched the windfall apples and pears piled high in the wooden bushel measure, is with me still. There were also damsons and plums to be selected for Mum's annual jam making and fruit bottling.

In August and September we picked fruit in the Wild Park. The blackberries were for pies and jam and the elderberries for homemade wine. We three girls spent hours away from home, exploring the Wild Park. It really lived up to its name then; there were no fields in the valley or Sports Pavilion. A park-keeper had a hut among the bushes, and once he let his huge black and brown dog out. It leapt up at me, knocking me flying and sending me bowling down the hillside. I have been wary of large black and brown dogs ever since.

On the east side of the Lewes Road, there were no buildings beyond the end of the Highway. There was farmland where the Schools now stand. Up at the top of The Avenue, when the builder's rubble was finally replaced by a landscaped green, with shrubs and small trees at each corner, some tennis-courts were laid out for the use of the residents. After Colbourne and Southall Avenues, The Crescent and Hillside were added to the estate, the numbers of children rapidly increased. We lived there with no play-parks, no schools, no church, no community centre.

The children walked miles to their schools. My sisters were

allowed to continue at their former Junior School, Ditchling Road, now called The Downs. Other children were placed in Coombe Road Schools. Some children who had moved here from outside Brighton were even less fortunate. As local schools became over-crowded, they had to walk to Falmer Village School. There were no school meals provided. Usually the children were sent home in the dinner hour and the school gates were often locked between 12 o'clock and 2 pm. My sisters had to carry their lunch to school, and then at dinnertime walk to a relative's house in Crescent Road, who allowed them to eat in her kitchen.

Despite our feelings of isolation, the baker and the milkman called daily at our doors. In the early days, Howard Barling and his brother started a milk round with a little cart and a churn, with brass pint and half-pint measures hanging on the side.

Then Mr Riches, a dairyman, came to live in Hillside with his wife and children, Morton and Joan, who were school contemporaries of mine. His round operated for many years, until the demands of modern hygiene made the Co-operative Dairy, with its bottled pasteurised milk, more popular. I remember my parents having serious discussions about the advantages and disadvantages of pasteurisation. It seemed to be a debate of major importance. Mr Hyder, our Co-op milkman, was a local man who lived with his family in North Moulsecoomb. Mrs Hyder was a popular and hardworking "pillar of the church", well known for her good works.

The first attempts at community life were centred around a wooden hut with a tin roof, in Hillside, which served as Church, Village Hall and Sunday School. First Mr Hurd, then the Reverend Carpenter were in charge of our welfare. We all joined the Church as it was the only recreational facility available outside the home - that is, all except my Dad who described himself as a free-thinker, having broken away in his teens from the demands of a strict Baptist upbringing. He was of the left in his political views, but was not a member of a trade union. He voted Labour and was a reader of the *Daily Herald*, and an admirer of Ramsay Macdonald and his cabinet. However, he let Mum have her own way about our religious upbringing, without too many grumbles. I remember some occasions on which they crossed swords, and of course, he never allowed any of us to be baptised until we were old enough to make up our own minds on the matter.

Later, more recreational facilities were provided at Moulsecoomb Place, when a Men's Club was opened, and much later a small Branch Library. Money was too short for Dad to join in any social activities. Good schooling for his girls was his first priority, so when Irene won a Hedgecock Scholarship soon after we moved to The Avenue, there was the expense of school uniform to consider.

For Irene there was an even longer walk to York Place each day, as there were no buses running to Brighton. York Place was the site of the original Grammar School before it moved to Varndean, Ditchling Road. Our only transport was a tram which ran from the barracks, the terminus being near where the present transport depot stands. But my sister usually walked, to save her penny fare. Four years later, Kathleen, my second sister, moved from Ditchling Road, to Balfour Road Senior Girls School, so she had an even longer walk to school. By this time, in 1926, I had started at Coombe Road Infants School, but only for a few weeks, as a bad attack of whooping cough kept me at home until after Easter. I can still remember the distress of that illness, and also of being taken to the Clinic at one time, because diptheria was suspected. I was told to open my mouth and a large spatula was inserted and a swab taken, while I coughed and choked, quite terrified by the whole experience.

I disliked my early schooldays, for my long absence made me feel quite ignorant when flash-cards with apples or buckets were held up to the class. I was miserable in the playground because I was a fat child whom the boys loved to chase and torment. By the time I was six and allowed to walk home from Coombe Road on my own, I was once chased along Dewe Road and into the path of a huge van. I can still see the driver's angry face as he shouted down at me, and I picked myself up, luckily only bruised. Of course I never told Mum, but another mother made it her business to do so, and I promised to be more careful.

I must have been a timid child, for we had to pass an old house with a high fence all round it at the end of Dewe Road, and when the boys told me that a witch lived there, I believed them. I always ran for my life past that fence and half-way up Southall Avenue. Perhaps these experiences helped me to lose some of my puppy-fat by the time I was seven, but they did not endear me to big boys. On another occasion my top and whip were snatched from me and thrown into the road. I ran to retrieve them into the path of a cyclist, and on this occasion got off with only a torn coat and wet pants. But at the age of seven all was changed. Some rooms at Moulsecoomb Place were turned into classrooms for the children aged seven to eleven, and after that, education really took off for me, and I loved every day. I shall save these reminiscences for Chapter Four.

Chapter II

FAMILY LIFE

The great thing about my Mum was that she was always there and ready to listen, and the back door was never locked - in fact it often stood wide open in summer. The great thing about my Dad was that although he was sometimes late home from work, he was there every evening, a stable presence, eating his tea long after us, and then doing his household jobs before settling in his chair with a book. His newspaper, The Daily Herald, was usually read at the breakfast table, folded in half and propped against the marmalade jar. This was how I acquired the useful habit of reading print upside-down. It has since proved a good standby during an interview, or even at the Doctor's surgery. I liked my Mum and Dad very much.

If I try to give a description of Mum as I saw her when a young girl, I would say that the most vivid feature of her face was the colour of her eyes. They were bright blue and often full of laughter. She had a mass of light brown wavy hair which she wore in a bun at the nape of her neck. She was of medium height , fairly slim, strong and active, I remember her being ill only once when I was young. She had a bright lively voice and was always singing about the house as she worked. I never saw her dance, but she was naturally athletic, and liked to share in the activities at Sunday School outings. It usually finished-up with Mum working herself up on the swing until she nearly flew over the top, while I stood by watching, scared and miserable. My Dad called her "Em", her sisters "Emmie", though she was christened "Emmeline", the eldest daughter in a family of nine children, eight of whom survived. She was the most unselfish person I knew, and loved us all. She showed it by slaving away to keep us and the house spotless and could never do enough for us. Her life was entirely centred round the home and our activities.

She had a proverb for every occasion. "A little help is worth a lot of pity", she quipped when we lent a hand in the kitchen. For an anticipated pleasure we heard the warning "Don't count your chickens until they are hatched". For a lost or broken possession our comfort was "It's no use crying over spilt milk". For a sisterly squabble we were reminded that "Least said is soonest mended". Enthusiasm had to be tempered by "Don't put all your eggs in one basket". Even my sister Kathleen carried on the tradition with her favourite saying "If a thing's worth doing it's worth doing well". With such pearls of wisdom was my pathway strewn.

She gave up attending church functions when she found that they demanded too much of her housekeeping money, but she saw that her girls were regular in their commitments. She seemed to obtain her pleasure from listening to the accounts of our day's adventures, round the kitchen table. She taught more by example than direction, and there was a constant atmosphere about the home of being busy and not wasting time. She travelled no further than Brighton, to shop once a week. She went away only twice when I was young and that was to attend a funeral first of her father and then her mother in Reading. In my middle teens I recall that she tried taking a holiday with Kathleen and some church friends, while I kept house for Dad. It was not for her, and she was home after a few days. She was a wise old woman and often gave her grandchildren advice *when it was asked.* They don't make 'em like that nowadays!

My Dad was never demonstrative, but I always remember the nods and smiles of approval he gave me. Later when there was homework to do, he was always ready with a correct spelling or a suggestion for the right word to express my meaning. Words were his business and good style seemed to come naturally to him. Books were our regular present from him, and he inscribed the fly-leaf with his elaborate script. He was naturally artistic and also musical. He told me that when he lived in Park Crescent as a teenager, he spent so much time hanging round the door of Congress Hall listening to the Salvation Army Band practice, that they put a cornet in his hand and asked him to join them.

In later years he bought a couple of mandolines, during his travels abroad, and they were lovely looking instruments with their dark polished wood bowls and mother of pearl decorations. By peering into the bowl, Napoli and the maker's Italian name could be deciphered. He sat many an hour playing plaintive folk melodies and the sound of that instrument when heard on the radio still brings tears to my eyes. When my sister Kathleen showed musical ability he gave her his second mandoline and taught her to play. She favoured Irish melodies, including the "Londonderry Air". She had strong hands and could press down those brassy wires, though it gave her corns on her fingertips. I tried once or twice, but gave up when it hurt my fingers.

The 1920s were a comparatively stable time for our family. Even the General Strike of 1926 did not affect us directly, apart from the fact that Dad had stones thrown at him on his way to work in Robert Street, because he was not a member of a trade union. He was a colour-printer and did book illustrations. He had only one week off a year and then he lost his pay. His basic pay was £3.10s a week but he could earn more with overtime. Sometimes there was a "rush job" such as the printing of the Brighton Guide, and the overtime would be saved for his week's holiday.

But he was more fortunate than some, as I was to discover when I talked to my fellow-scholarship-winners. Kathleen's Dad in The Highway could earn only £2.10s a week as a railway man and her Mum went out to work doing cleaning, in order to keep two children at Grammar Schools. Dorothy's father in Hillside, we children considered quite wealthy, because he was a commercial artist who earned £5 a week. Rita's father in Hillside must have been wealthy also, because although we did not know his salary as a commercial traveller, he actually ran a car, and took his family of four children out and about. How we envied them. My Mum did not go out to work to keep Irene and me at Grammar Schools, but she took in paying guests, usually relatives from Reading, every summer. They had our little sitting room and the big bedroom above. Mum and Dad made do on the double bed in the spare room and we three girls were in the other front bedroom.

My Dad worked long hours, from 7.30 a.m. till 5.30 or 6 p.m. He walked to work along the Lewes Road to Robert Street, then back for his dinner, and then did the double journey in the afternoon. He had such a short dinner break, that the meal had to be in front of him the moment he stepped in the door, and even then, his after-dinner cup of tea was usually drunk standing up or saucered for quicker cooling. He used to like a pint of beer and a pipe of tobacco when he was young, but he gave these up, as expenses grew. All his interests were centred round his home and family.

My Mum backed him up, working hard in the house, cooking, cleaning, polishing and washing. I remember the white sheets and the white counterpanes, as well as our dresses. Washing seemed to go on all day on a Monday, and I hated Monday dinner with cold meat and potatoes. It always seemed to be full of the smell of soapsuds.

Mum sang all the time she was working, sometimes it was a hum, sometimes a full-throated rendering of an Edwardian Music Hall song. She had a good singing voice, and in her late teens, when she helped her parents run their public house in Reading, she used to sing to the gentlemen in the back-parlour on a Saturday night. So I learnt the words of many an old Music Hall Song, though sometimes if she thought I was listening, she hummed through the "naughty bits". So if anyone should care to listen, I can still give a rendering of such old favourites as "Put on your tata little girlie", "By the light of the silvery moon", "Roaming in the gloaming", "There was I waiting at the church", "Two little girls in blue", "The soldiers of the Queen" and many more. One song I can never sing now is Harry Lauder's "Keep right on to the end of the road", as that was what Mum sang to Dad during the last painful weeks of his final illness.

We were also reared on classical overtures and Grand Opera, and became familiar with the voices of Clara Butt and Maggie Teyte, or Caruso and Peter Dawson. Dad had an old second-hand wind-up gramophone with a green horn, and he enjoyed many a winter Saturday afternoon listening to his classical records which he bought cheap from Edwards Music Shop in London Road. Sometimes the gramophone spring broke because he overwound it, and then with much tut-tutting, he would spread newspaper all over our round Victorian dining table, and take the whole machine to bits. The coiled spring was finally replaced, having been somewhat shortened, which meant that he had to be even more cautious about winding it. Sometimes the black and gold classical shaped mantlepiece clock would stop, and then there was a major crisis since none of us had watches and there was no radio. Usually the whole clock was taken to pieces on the table, and I was not allowed to touch anything. My Dad always grumbled and I was so relieved when the old clock was back in place and we could all relax.

The other job which I was always pleased to see completed was shoe repairing. How he must have hated that Saturday afternoon job in the back scullery, though I never actually heard him grumble. He kept all five of us well shod, and we never went to a cobbler. He bought pieces of leather from a shop on the corner of Sydney Street and Trafalgar Street, bending them between his hands and examining their thickness. Then back home, out came the last and hammer, the tacks and clasp knife from the cupboard under the stairs, and he would be out there for ages, shaping and cutting, then hammering, with the gilt tacks held in readiness between his teeth. Finally came the unmistakable smell of the heel-ball, and then I knew that the job was nearly done, and Mum could begin to get the tea. Sometimes there would be gramophone records after tea, until such time as he bought his first EKCO radio, and then the old favourites were neglected, in favour of Mantovani and his Orchestra, or music from the Palm Court.

However hard Mum tried, the housekeeping money never seemed to stretch quite far enough, and of course she prided herself on never having anything on tick, not like some of her neighbours with their London ways! So on Fridays we children went a bit short of food so that Dad could have a good meal in front of him. This meant that we had a bowl of bread soaked in Oxo gravy before he came home, or just an egg. Once when Mum was short of money, she sent me down to the local shop to buy one egg. Of course I played tricks on the way back and dropped it. "There", she said "I've no more money, you'll have to pay for it out of your money box." So back I had to go with my tail between my legs. That taught me a lesson.

Dad had to work on Saturday mornings till one o'clock before he got his pay. Before one o'clock we were all waiting for him with empty shopping baskets on the door of the print shop, smelling the familiar scent of the ink and listening to the rattle of the machines. When Dad appeared with his pay packet it did not stay in his pocket very long. We were off on our tour of the back streets, for meat and vegetables. I remember the rare treat of an icecream from the Hokey Pokey Man in Kensington Gardens. Sometimes in Trafalgar Street Dad called into the herbalist's to buy a lump of licorice for sore throats, or a drink called Sarsaparilla, or some other herbal remedy. We never went to doctors, because we could not afford them. A winter cold was treated by eating a raw onion, and by rubbing the chest with camphorated oil. A glass of hot homemade elderberry wine was another winter remedy very much enjoyed when I had a cough.

We called in Eltenton's Grocery on the corner of Trafalgar Street and York Place, then on to Edward's Music Shop to listen to the latest tune belting out. It might be "K-k-k-Katy" or at another time "Aint it grand to be blooming well dead". On one such occasion as we stood laughing by the open door, one of my Dad's strictly religious cousins came by and saw us. She passed on in disgust, and Dad and Mum had a laugh together. The next stop was always at the blacksmith's in Marshall Row, and even if we were not lucky enough to see a shoeing, there was always plenty of clanging and clattering and a good red fire.

Once inside the Open Market, with the lights flaring on the stalls, and everyone shouting his wares, all was noise and confusion. We searched for later afternoon bargains, such as bunches of ripe bananas or cheap blood oranges. Occasionally there was a catch of local herrings and we could buy them at four for a penny. Sometimes Dad bought winkles for Sunday tea, or some bloaters to have for our Saturday meal. As we had not eaten since breakfast time we were always famished. We stopped for sweets at cousin Jack's market stall. He sold a very good line in slab toffee I remember, and our Dad used to break it up with a little hammer and store it in a jar well out of our reach.

However hungry we were, (and we still had the long walk to face along the Lewes Road to Moulsecoomb) we had to make one more stop at Speaker's Corner which was on the side of the Level facing the Open Market. It operated on Saturdays and was just like a mini Hyde Park, where anyone with opinions to express could stand on a soap box. One of these was often my Dad's brother, Dick, with his radical political views. Uncle Dick was one of the old school of idealistic Communists. He was also a pacifist in the First World War and was sent to prison where he went on a hunger strike. He was a keen worker for the Brighton Co-operative Movement and was on the Committee of Management. He taught young people in the Education Department of the Co-op. He also went to Russia as a delegate more than once.

Dad loved to stand and listen, and indeed Dick was a great spell-binder, but I found it all distinctly embarrassing, because I loved Uncle Dick and felt he was making a show of himself. I remember myself as hanging behind and trailing my fingers along the dirty green railings in Gladstone Place, and being told to pick my feet up.

We always had something nice cooked for tea, and then came the weekly routine of hair washing and baths. As we all three had thick hair, and mine was particularly curly, it must have been quite a performance for Mum, as I always made a song and dance about having my hair attended to. Bath-time was singing time for Kathleen, who had a particularly fine voice, so we were well entertained until Dad shouted up the stairs that he had had enough, and she was to "pack it up".

Outdoor play was usually ball games in the back garden, or skipping. Indoors, we played imaginative games such as "holidays", which meant pulling out Dad's old leather trunk from the cupboard and turning the spare bed into a train or a boat. Kathleen favoured "mothers and fathers", but Irene got bored with that. We played "schools" interminably, using the well-worn blackboard and easel. As I was so much younger than my sisters I was always the pupil who did not know anything. Fear of being a dunce drove me to recite my tables and to learn my parts of speech in English Grammar long before I heard of them at school.

When my sisters were older, they went their own ways without me. They both had bicycles, but I only had a wooden scooter, so I played alone, or with the girl next door. Then their various church activities took them away from home a great deal, and I was left with the company of my parents. They were great readers and members of the Moulsecoomb Public Library, so I became the same, and my Dad in particular guided my reading during those formative years.

Dad's holidays from work consisted of one week a year of unpaid leave, plus Bank Holidays. So every day off meant a treat for the family. We walked to Stanmer Park, Ditchling Beacon, Falmer Pond or Rottingdean and took a huge picnic in the well of the pram, which included plates, cups, bottles and cutlery. This meant that Mum stayed up half the night, baking and preparing this massive family picnic, so that we could get off to an early start. Even then it never seemed early enough for Dad, who used to grumble reproachfully when it was fine weather, saying "Emmie, can't you leave all that?"

In August our picnics took on a more purposeful air, as we were expected to fill the empty picnic baskets with dandelions, elderberries, or blackberries, in preparation for Mum's winemaking and jam making. I hated these trips when I was small, as I was left strapped in the pram and told I was minding the picnic, while the family, so it seemed, disappeared in the bushes for ever. I became frantic and used to shout "Coo-ee" continually, waiting for an answering cry. When my big sisters grew up and had their own interests, Dad went off on his blackberrying trips alone, sometimes as far as Mary Farm. He would be gone all day, returning in triumph with his two wicker shopping baskets laden with black juicy fruit, and decorated with wreaths of wild honeysuckle .

Every year in August, Dad bought Mum a new summer hat ready for the Bank Holiday outing. So wet Bank Holidays were black days, as Mum came home bad tempered with a ruined floppy hat, and we were all as miserable as the weather. But often the sun shone, so we walked to the seafront, and watched the antics of the London daytrippers disgorging from their coaches, or char-a-bancs, as they were called. Then we went on the Palace Pier, but were not allowed to waste money on the slot machines, so we never knew what the butler saw, and besides the view-finder was placed too high to peer into.

However, some of the animated theatre scenes such as "The

Haunted House" were free for all to see. There was a palmist and a stunt-man, who dived through flames into the sea. There was a tearoom and an orchestra, a family show in the theatre, and ballroom dancing behind screens at the end of the Palace Pier, near the jetty where the paddlesteamers came in. On rare occasions Dad took us all on the steamer to Eastbourne or the Isle of Wight, and I still remember the excitement of clattering down the iron steps of the landing stage, with the siren sounding full blast. I found seats for the family but could never stay in mine for long. I was up at the rail, or down below watching the shiny turning paddles, with Dad trailing behind to keep an eye on me.

During our school summer holidays we spent every sunny day on Dalton's Beach. Dad came down and joined us in his dinner hour and had a quick swim with us before eating his picnic. He was a good swimmer and entertained us with his somersaults and underwater dives. He taught me confidence in the sea, as well as respect for its power. No on talked about pollution in those days and much more was said about the benefits of ozone and seabathing. Mum never got any further than paddling with her skirts tucked up into her waistband, but she loved the seaside.

The coming of cold Autumn days, meant, in our family, Christmas preparations. It began with the making of the jams, pickles and wines. I can still remember the comfort of a glass of hot wine, sitting drinking it by our kitchen range, while Mum took a hot brick out of the oven and wrapped it in a piece of old blanket, in preparation for my ascent up the cold staircase to the unheated bedroom. Then came the buying of all the "extras" for Christmas each week, as money would allow. Next came the laborious process of preparing the nuts and fruits for the puddings and cakes. It was a question of "many hands make light work" with so much to be done. All dried fruit was unwashed and unsorted, and sometimes small foreign bodies, such as pieces of stone could be found. Then the fruit had to be washed and dried carefully on flat trays. The candied peel was bought in great lumps, with sugar adhering to it, to be chopped by hand laboriously. The almonds were sold whole, in the outer skins, which were often very difficult to remove. We soaked them in cups of boiling water, before getting our busy fingers to work. The culmination of all these efforts came with the stirring of the Christmas pudding mixture, when each of us made an unspoken wish. My Mum's puddings were good, so were her Christmas cakes. She decorated the cakes with crystallised fruits because she liked her decorations to be edible.

Every December a second Christmas cake arrived by parcel post from Aunty Sis, my Dad's sister, who was married to a caterer from Tunbridge Wells. She and her husband owned a Bakery and Confectioner's, and later, a hotel, but they never forgot their various nieces and nephews. I can still recall the anticipation as we waited for the parcel strings to be cut. Inside, beautifully wrapped, and placed around the edges of the box, were little parcels of home made sweets, chocolates and cakes and biscuits.

In the centre stood the cake, and such a cake! fit for a bride I used to think, as I gazed at the pretty shell edgings all in white icing. Only the dainty holly trimmings betrayed its true function, as a birthday cake in memory of Christ. We always had to reassure Mum that hers was the better one.

My parents kept up the Father Christmas charade for many years, and my sisters played along with them all the time I was small. So I was a school girl before I discovered that Santa with the strange hollow and booming voice was Dad talking through our old green gramophone horn, and that the muffled squeaks and gasps from below came from Mum who was splitting her sides with laughter and stuffing her apron in her mouth. We were threatened by the knowledge that there would be no presents if we jumped out of bed, but as soon as we heard Mum's "Well goodbye Father Christmas" and the bang of the front door, we leapt first to the front window, then to the back bedroom window, but we never saw him. Our gifts were few and small, but we loved them, and there was always a big book from Dad.

Our more extravagant gifts came later in the day, because we always spent Christmas Day at the house of Uncle Dick and Auntie Avis in Hampstead Road. They had no children and were comfortably off, so every year they invited his brothers and their wives and various nieces and nephews to a grand party. Uncle Dick always wore fancy dress; one year he would be a postman and come in with a huge sack on his back. That was the time I picked out a lovely-golden haired doll from his sack. Sometimes he would dress as Santa Claus and pretend to appear from the chimney. His most uncomfortable year must have been when he rigged up a sort of fish pond and crouched beneath it, hooking presents on to fishing lines, completely hidden from view. How he managed to hook the right presents on to the right lines I shall never know, but I remember Mum pulling up a most handsome sewing basket for herself.

We played balloon hand-ball in two teams across a long dining room table, and we played guessing games, and then sometimes my cousin Bernard and I would kneel up at the front window, watching the trains at Preston Park Station. If my memory is not faulty, there must have been trains running over Christmas in those days. Uncle Dick's party was the highlight of our year, not even dimmed by the long trek home in the dark, with the gifts piled in the pushchair and me perched on my Dad's shoulders for part of the journey.

New Year brought with it the promise of our annual visit to the Panto at "The Grand" in North Road, now the site of the Brighthelm Centre. We queued as soon as Dad came out of work on Saturday, and filled ourselves with hot saveloys from the cookshop across the road. One pantomine song I remember from *Aladdin* goes:

> "Put your worries through the mangle

Like Mother does on washing day.
When you're in an awful tangle
Wash those blues away.
Though the sun is shining through the window pane
When mother hangs the washing out it always rains
So-o-o ... put your worries through the mangle...".

Another recalled incident is of a couple of clowns holding a too-short plank across too-wide trestles, and singing:

"It's a little bit too short,
Turn it round the other way".

to the tune of "In a Monastery Garden". We thought it hilarious! Another pantomine tune of that era was:

"Chick chick chick chick chicken
Lay a little egg for me.
Chick chick chick chick chicken
I want one for my tea.
I haven't had an egg since Easter
And now it's half-past three.
S-o-o... chick chick chick etc".

But the highlight of every show was surely the slapstick comedy act with the bucket of whitewash and brushes. I would watch the clowns' antics with mixed feelings of consternation and delight.

There was consternation in seeing nice clean clothes and walls being defaced, and there was delight in witnessing such naughtiness going unchecked and being applauded. Finally my scruples were overcome, giving way to joy and laughter when the contents of the bucket were deposited over the poor clown's head, while he clawed pathetically at his face to reveal two strange white-rimmed eyes.

This cartoon in *The Housing Reformer* just after World War One shows a humble working man facing "the choice" between the misery of city slums and the health and happiness of a garden suburb which would be an "insurance against bolshevism" and keep the workers docile. South Moulsecoomb, built in the early twenties, was hailed as a Utopia. But only artisans and professional workers, many from outside Brighton, could afford the high rents.

The Avenue, taken from the Lewes Road about 1930. Ruby's house, number eight, is third from the right.

When South Moulsecoomb was built, the area belonged to the Parish of Patcham in the Rural District of Steyning East. The boundaries of the then County Borough of Brighton were extended in 1923 to take in the new estate. In the document below Patcham Parish signs over its territorial rights to Brighton.

COPY OF RESOLUTION

passed at a Meeting of the

PATCHAM PARISH COUNCIL

held on the 28th day of November, 1922.

A letter was read from the Brighton Town Council submitting copy of Resolution passed by them on the question of extending the boundaries of the area of the Council to include the Moulsecoomb Housing Estate, Patcham, and after consideration thereof it was resolved that the Parish Council do not oppose the application of the Town Council and that the Town Council be informed accordingly.

(Signed) JOSEPH HARRIS,
Clerk to the Patcham Parish Council.

Tram and Bus Timetable from the Official Brighton Corporation Guide of 1935-36. Printed by the Southern Publishing Company where Ruby's father was employed.

INDEX TO TRANSPORT ROUTES.

CORPORATION TRAMS.

Service No. and Through Fare		Frequency (in mins.)	Route.
L	1½d.	4.	**SEA FRONT (AQUARIUM) and MOULSECOOMB** *via* Marlborough Place, Glo'ster Place, St. Peter's Church, Lewes Road.
E	2d.	10.	**SEA FRONT (AQUARIUM)** and **ELM GROVE** and **RACE HILL** *via* Route L to St. Peter's Church, Waterloo Place, Elm Grove.
Q	2d.	10.	**SEA FRONT (AQUARIUM)** and **QUEEN'S PARK** *via* Route E to Junction Elm Grove (Junction of Queen's Park Road) thence to Lower Rock Gardens.
***D**	2d.	4.	**SEA FRONT (AQUARIUM)** and **DITCHLING ROAD** *via* Route L to St. Peter's Church, Ditchling Road, Preston Drove (Municipal Golf Links and Hollingbury Camp.
***B**	2d.	4.	**SEA FRONT (AQUARIUM)** and **BEACONSFIELD ROAD** *via* Route L to St. Peter's Church, London Road, Preston Circus, Beaconsfield Road and Villas, Preston Drove.
N	2d.	5.	**SEA FRONT (AQUARIUM)** and **DYKE ROAD** *via* Route B to Preston Circus, New England Road, Seven Dials, Dyke Road.
C	2d.	5.	**SEVEN DIALS** and **LOWER ROCK GARDENS** and **RACE HILL** *via* New England Road, Preston Circus, College, Elm Grove to Race Hill and Queen's Park Road to Lower Rock Gardens.
S	1d.	5.	**SEA FRONT** and **CENTRAL STATION** *via* Marlborough Place, North Road, Queen's Road.
2d. from Station to any part of tram system.			*Note: Routes D and B comprise a Circular Tour of over 4 miles, occupying 30 minutes.

TILLINGS BUSES (Summer Service).

Service No. and Through Fare		Frequency (in mins.)	Route.
1.	6d.	7½.	**PORTSLADE STATION** and **WHITEHAWK** (Lintott Avenue) *via* New Church Road, Western Road, North Street. St. James's Street, St. George's Road, Chesham Road, Eastern Road, Sussex Square, Whitehawk Road (returning *via* Bristol Gardens).
2.	8d.	7½. (to Race Hill) 22. (to Woodingd'n)	**PORTSLADE STATION** and **RACE HILL** and **WOODINGDEAN** (Downs Hotel) *via* Portland Road, Blatchington Road, Norton Road, Church Road, Western Road, North Street, Marine Parade, Lower and Upper Rock Gardens, Edward Street, Freshfield Road, Warren Road. On Race Days buses run every few minutes from Old Steine. On Sundays every 10 minutes to Woodingdean.
2A	5d.	64. (Weekdays)	**ROTTINGDEAN** and **WOODINGDEAN** and **RACE HILL** *via* High Street, Falmer Road, Downs Road, Warren Road. On Sundays buses run every 20 minutes between Rottingdean and Woodingdean only.
3.	4d.	8.	**HOVE STATION** and **ARUNDEL ROAD** *via* Goldstone Villas, Ventnor Villas, Church Road, Western Road, North Street, St. James's Street, St. George's Road, Chesham Road, Sussex Square.
4.	10d.	12.	**SOUTHWICK GREEN** and **ROTTINGDEAN** *via* Southview Road, Old Shoreham Road, Boundary Road, Portland Road, Sackville Road, Church Road, Western Road, North Street, Marine Parade, Arundel Road, Roedean Road, Marine Drive.
4A	5d.	50.	**OLD STEINE** and **OVINGDEAN** *via* Marine Parade, Arundel Road, Roedean Road, Greenways.
5.	8d.	20.	**WEST HOVE** (Elm Drive) and **PATCHAM FOUNTAIN** *via* Elm Drive, Old Shoreham Road, Sackville Road, Church Road, Western Road, North Street, Victoria Gardens, London Road, Preston Road.

5B	**8d.**	**10.**	**PORTSLADE STATION** and **LADIES MILE ESTATE** (The Deeside) *via* Carlton Terrace, Old Shoreham Road, Sackville Road, Church Road, Western Road, North Street, Victoria Gardens, London Road, Preston Road, Carden Avenue, Winfield Avenue, Mackie Avenue.
6.	**4d.**	**7.**	**FISHERSGATE** and **BRIGHTON STATION** *via* Eastbrook Road, St. Andrew's Road, New Church Road, Western Road, Queen's Road, Surrey Street.
6A	**8d.**	**10.**	**PORTSLADE STATION** (South Entrance) and **PORTSLADE STATION** (North Entrance) *via* Boundary Road, Kingsway, Hove Street, Church Road, Western Road, Queen's Road, Surrey Street, Brighton Station, Buckingham Place, Dyke Road, Old Shoreham Road, Carlton Terrace.
7.	**6d.**	**20.** (from Portslade) **5.** (from Hove Statn.)	**PORTSLADE STATION** and **HOVE STATION** and **ARUNDEL ROAD** (Kemp Town) *via* Portland Road, Sackville Road, Blatchington Road, Goldstone Villas, Hove Station, Cromwell Road, Davigdor Road, Buckingham Place, Brighton Station, Queen's Road, North Street, St. James's Street, Bristol Road, Chesham Road, Eastern Road, Sussex Square, Arundel Road.
8.	**7d.**	**20.**	**DYKE ROAD** and **HOLLINGBURY** (Preston Drove) *via* Upper Drive, Old Shoreham Road, Dyke Road, Seven Dials, Vernon Terrace, Montpelier Road, Western Road, Preston Street, King's Road, Old Steine, Victoria Gardens, London Road, Preston Road, Harrington Road, Loder Road, Balfour Road, Ditchling Road, Municipal Golf Links.
8A	**7d.**	**20.**	**DYKE ROAD** and **HOLLINGBURY** (Surrenden Road) *via* same route as Service 8.
8B	**1d.**	**15.** (rush hours only)	**OLD SHOREHAM ROAD** (Grammar School) and **SEA FRONT** (Preston Street) *via* Dyke Road, Seven Dials, Vernon Terrace, Montpelier Road, King's Road, (returning *via* Preston Street, Western Road, Montpelier Road, Seven Dials, Dyke Road, Highdown Road, Wolstonbury Road).
9.	**3d.**	**30.**	**PORTSLADE STATION** and **MILE OAK** *via* Victoria Road, Southern Cross, Locks Hill, Upper Portslade. On Sunday, Wednesday, Friday and Saturday afternoons every 15 minutes.
10.	**2d.**	**Irregular**	**PORTSLADE STATION** and **HOVE STATION** *via* Boundary Road, New Church Road, Sackville Road, Blatchington Road, Goldstone Villas (Mornings and Evenings only, Saturdays and Sundays excepted, for connection with certain London trains).
11.	**2d.**	**15.**	**PRESTON CIRCUS** and **COOMBE ROAD** (for Brighton Sanatorium) *via* Viaduct Road, Upper Lewes Road, Lewes Road, Coombe Road, Baden Road (returning *via* Shaftesbury Road and Stanley Road, instead of Viaduct Road).
13.	**4d.**	**15.**	**HOVE STADIUM** and **BRIGHTON STATION** *via* Nevill Road, Sackville Road, Hove Street, Kingsway, King's Road, West Street, Queen's Road, Surrey Street.
14.	**6d.**	**15.**	**BOUNDARY ROAD** (Seaford Road, Hove) and **LEWES ROAD** *via* Kingsway, Hove Street, Church Road, Holland Road, Davigdor Road, Montefiore Road, Old Shoreham Road, Upper Drive, Highcroft Villas, Dyke Road Drive, Stanford Avenue, Hollingbury Crescent and Place, Roedale Road, Hollingdean Road.

During the Summer Months, on fine days, additional buses work on several routes.

Latest information concerning routes and times, etc., can be found in the current bus map and time table obtainable from the Company's officials or at the Local Office, Conway Street, Hove. Telephone—HOVE 1002-3

SPECIAL DAILY LATE BUSES FROM BRIGHTON STATION.

Service 6.—12 midnight to **FISHERSGATE** *via* New Church Road.

Service 6.—1 a.m. to **PORTSLADE STATION** *via* New Church Road.

Service 7.—12 midnight, 1 a.m., to **ARUNDEL ROAD.**

Service 2.—1 a.m. to **PORTSLADE STATION** *via* Portland Road (Wednesday and Saturday nights only).

Moulseccomb Place: Ruby's first school after moving to the estate, where no school was built until 1927. **Above**: the entrance. **Below**: Mr Vic Taylor's class was held at the back, in the Mediaeval part of the building which is the oldest in Brighton.

The original St Andrews Church, South Moulsecoomb, which lost its spire and became a Parish Hall when it was replaced in the 1930s by a fine brick and stone built church with adjoining vicarage.

The new Moulsecoomb Schools, built in the late twenties and early thirties. In1929 the Juniors were housed with the Infants in the right-hand wing of the top building, which then stood on its own.

Chapter III

NEIGHBOURS AND SOCIAL LIFE

Our neighbours in The Avenue were such interesting people, and some of them I have kept in touch with to this day. My Dad used to enjoy talking to them, because they came from different walks of life and few of them were Brightonians. So great had been the publicity for this new Garden Suburb, that advertisements appeared in the London Press. At a time when new houses were in such short supply, people were prepared to move into them from other towns, and some of the menfolk living in The Avenue were commuting to London, I remember. My Dad must have had his share of yarns to swop over the garden fence, since he had travelled round the world twice since the age of twenty one, on his way to Australia and then to New Zealand. He had not married until his late thirties, and was at that time about fifty. He had black wavy hair, and a fuzz of black on his chest and arms, and was nicknamed "Tarzan" by the local lads.

My first close contact with neighbours was with another Mr and Mrs Taylor whose garden in Southall Avenue backed on ours. He was a Civil Servant and she had been a school teacher, and they had no children, so appeared to "adopt" me for much of the time before I started school. I played in their garden and rode on the back of Gyp, their black sheepdog. I remember being taken out to a teashop, or to visit Father Christmas at Stafford's, by Mrs Taylor. Staffords was a large department store standing on the present site of the South Eastern Electricity Board in Western Road (1990). There was a restaurant on the first floor where tea dances were held. These were pleasures unknown to my sisters, because money was so short.

Then I remember Mr and Mrs Cook at No 12, because Barbara Cook was my first friend, and when her sister Phyllis was born, my Mum looked after Mrs Cook and Barbara came to stay with us. When I was nine, Mr Cook's Civil Service post was moved to Kent, the family moved and I was sad. Mrs Cook had made us promise we would write to each other, and we have done so ever since, even though Barbara's married life has taken her to Jamaica and the Southern United States. We had a reunion in my house very recently.

The most lasting contact has been with the French family who moved into No 6 The Avenue at the same time as us, because I still keep in touch with the remaining members of that family today. There were Eric and Marie who were young adults, and Yvonne who was the same age as myself. It was in fact only their father who was French, and I loved his accent, his courtly manners, and his smart suit and silver-topped cane. He played the piano in a most accomplished manner, and whenever I heard the familiar strains of "Nights of gladness" through the adjoining wall, I used to waltz around our living room singing "Oopsey doopsey daisy-o" in time to the melody.

Eric was musical too. He had a little wind-up gramophone and played "The Sun has got his hat on", or sometimes he would tap-dance on the bare floor to "Bye-bye blackbird". I thought he was like a filmstar, but he became in fact an Estate Agent. Marie was very pretty and worked at the Queen's Hotel. In later years when she was head housekeeper, she used to take me and Yvonne to Staff Dances at the Queen's Ballroom. I was overwhelmed with shyness, never having had a dancing lesson, but Marie jogged me happily round the room, not appearing to notice my discomfort.

Their mother, Mrs de Bretagne, was one of the kindest and most generous women I was ever to meet, and she helped me and my sisters in innumerable ways. She was an excellent dressmaker and milliner, so if it was a question of a costume for a school play, or a white dress for our confirmation, she was there at hand to help us. Her parties were something to be remembered too, and it always seemed that just as I was beginning to relax and enjoy myself, my Dad would be knocking with the poker on the kitchen wall; that was my signal to go home to bed and I was always the first to leave. On such occasions, I used to rate my parents as the strictest in the whole world.

Our neighbours at No 10 were the Townsends, a young couple

without any children. Mrs Townsend took me out into town sometimes, and I thought she was a lovely lady. Her husband worked in Local Government. They moved to Lewes after some years, leaving behind a mystery in my mind which was never cleared up. All I can remember is the whispering over the garden fences, and hearing "Took him in his car to Falmer, horsewhipped him and threw him in the pond." It sounded like a good story to me.

Across the wide green lived Mr and Mrs Meiklejohn with Jean and Munro. They owned Dalton's Bathing Station, and also ran the Amusement Arcade on the Palace Pier. We liked going to Dalton's Beach because it was clean and there were wooden boards to help you walk over the stones, and also there was more sand at low tide than on many beaches. Next door to them lived another Scottish couple named Mr and Mrs McEwen who had no children and didn't like cats either. In the days before the Walls Ice Cream "Stop Me and Buy One" tricycles appeared, they used to drive a smart van round our estate, selling halfpenny icecream cones and penny wafers. The wife perched in the back of the van, appeared a formidable figure to me, especially after one memorable day, when the van stopped outside our gate, and she shouted to me "Have yer got a yeller cat?" Thinking of my beloved Ginger Tom I nodded my head. "If he gets in my winder again I'll kill 'im", she threatened. Some years after, when my cat did in fact die, I was convinced that I knew the killer.

A few doors down from them lived a widow and former school teacher called Mrs Dawson, who helped in the Sunday School. She took in Miss Nicholls as a lodger, who was my teacher when I was eight. Further up the road on our side lived Mr Vic Taylor and later young Reg Burroughs. Across from them and higher still lived Mr Kitchen my Headmaster. All these worthy people taught me at various times, and were friends as well as teachers, all living together in this little community.

Then up the road on our side lived Mrs Richardson whose famous brother used to stay with her during the summer. This was none other than Mr Herbert Morrison a Labour Member of Parliament, who was later to obtain a Cabinet position in the Labour Government. My Dad used to point him out with pride, as we saw him striding past our house.

Billy and Joyce Whiting were at school with me and lived next to Mrs Richardson. Their Dad became a Town Councillor. So did Desmond Manton's Dad who lived in The Highway. Councillor Manton went one better and became a Brighton Alderman and had a road named after him.

Another class-mate of mine who received some small claim to fame, was Keith Rawlings who lived at the top of the road near the tennis courts. He was the Prince Charming to my Wicked Witch, in a school production of "The Sleeping Beauty". Little did I know then, that I was rubbing shoulders with a real live actor. He later trained under Madame Florence Moore, and after his stage career, he became Controller of Television on the island of Cyprus. I still hear news of him through a mutual friend and he has now retired to the Home Counties.

We also could claim a musical composer among the early residents of Hillside. My sister Kathleen remembers him because he always took large brown envelopes to our local Post Office to be stamped. Once when she was cycling near the shops, this man came running down the hill, stopped her, put some money in her hand, and asked her to post his brown envelope, then ran on. We only discovered the full significance of these brown envelopes in the last decade. This was when reading a musical biography of a British composer named Havergal Brian, we came upon a mention of Brighton and a photograph of his council house at Moulsecoomb. This could at once be identified as the house at 130 Hillside as we had known it. The regularly posted packets could be explained by the fact that, living as he did in poverty at that time, he supplemented his income by taking in hack-work, copying manuscripts. His last years were spent in a flat overlooking Shoreham Harbour, and he died recently at a great age. Musical experts have taken up his work, and there is now a Havergal Brian Society.

So much for famous sons of Moulsecoomb, not forgetting three of my schoolmates, who had lived within five minutes walk of my house, and who never survived the Second World War.

***

As mentioned earlier, there was a complete lack of social facilities on our new estate, and improvements came at a very slow rate. The Church took the initiative in this matter, and as soon as the first small St Andrew's Church was built, the tin hut became available as a Church Hall and could be booked for various functions, though it was mainly used by Church groups such as the Men's Club, Women's Union, Sunday School, Choir and Drama Groups, Brownies, Cubs, Guides and Scouts. The main feature of that little church of St Andrews was a plain chancel arch over which was inscribed in gold letters on brown wood: "Where two or three are gathered together in My name, there am I in the midst of them".

With the growth of the North Moulsecoomb Estate from 1926 to 1930, the tin hut became inadequate, and it was a great pleasure to have a new brick building, St George's Hall, built in North Moulsecoomb. This was due mainly to pressure from Moulsecoomb Ratepayers' Association headed by two worthy local men, Mr Kilner and Mr Bankes. Now the Church had two venues for its various functions, including services, for which the Hall had been consecrated. At the same time Moulsecoomb Junior and Infants School had been built, with its fine stretch of playing fields running down to the Lewes Road. Both Hall and fields could be hired for social functions, and this meant the main Church events such as the May Queen Celebrations and the

Summer Fete, with its competitive races and sideshows, tended to centre round St George's Hall as it was adjacent to the School Field. By 1931 a large section of these fields was lost, by the building of Moulsecoomb Secondary School.

Meanwhile on the hilltop behind South Moulsecoomb, Mr Braybon built an estate of private houses called Higher Bevendean Estate. No sooner was this completed, than the Brighton Corporation-owned land beyond Bevendean was swarming with another estate of small semi-detached houses called East Moulsecoomb, which started building in 1926. This Council development was part of Brighton Corporation's policy of house clearance, which proved so unsatisfactory for the uprooted Brighton families, but which was acclaimed by the Housing Department.

Even less thought appeared to be given to the provision of social facilities in East Moulsecoomb. Many residents were completely disorientated, living, as it seemed, isolated in the heart of the country with Hodshrove Farm on their doorsteps. This was a far cry from the cosy family life in the backstreets of Brighton, with Gran up the road and Mum across the way. Once again it was the Church, backed by the Ratepayers' Association, which made the first move with the building of St Francis Hall in Moulsecoomb Way. This too was consecrated for religious use, so that both services and lay meetings could be held. Sunday School classes were arranged in this Hall, and there were strong parish links between St George's, St Francis', and St Andrew's, with one

Vicar in charge. He needed to delegate work to his Curate and to a Church Army Captain, who was permanently with us for many years.

With this population explosion, tiny St Andrew's Church became quite inadequate, so the tin hut was pulled down, and on the site between it and the church, a fine new brick and stone church was built in the 1930s, with an adjoining Vicarage. Keir Hett of Ardingly, Sussex, was the architect, and it is a fine tribute to him. The former church, minus its spire, now became our Parish Hall. We were justly proud of our new light and airy Church, with its modern seating and simple altar, screened on each side by blue curtains. It was a functional building, for the curtains could be used to screen the altar completely, and the raised chancel could be used as a stage for drama productions. This phenomenon in church building is now accepted as the norm, but it was the first of its kind in this area.

It is not so easy to remember the names of all the church members in the early days, but some names still come to mind. There were the Tugwells, the Crooks, the Hallmarks, the Smiths, the Holdaways, the Fields, the Imms, the Rodbards, the Markwicks, the Mantons, the Marshs and the Taylors, the Balls, the Potters, the Kingslands and Williams.

The people in charge of our welfare can be vividly recalled. First, there was Mr Hurd in the tin hut, followed by the Reverend

Carpenter and the Reverend Berrington, who both had, one after the other, a council house in Hillside opposite the church, as their Vicarage. Miss Marjorie Tugwell was the Sunday School Superintendant and she also organised annual concerts in the hut. Later, Mrs Catt, a former teacher, started a choir; and Mr Percy Smith, who subsequently trained for the Ministry, organised an annual pantomime.

To the new church and vicarage came the Reverend Bransby Jones with his wife and daughter. He was a High Churchman with great musical ability. He introduced such innovations as robes, processions, incense, sung Mass, and the New English Hymnal, into our lives. We sang hymns with modern settings by Ralph Vaughan Williams and others. We were encouraged to perform religious dramas in the church, such as "The Upper Room" by Charles Williams. "The Boy With the Cart" by Christopher Fry, being the story of St Cuthman of Steyning, was also performed at this time. These changes were bound to prove unpopular with some older parishioners, but nevertheless the size of the congregation increased. The Vicar was unpopular for another reason. Just before the outbreak of the Second World War, he preached pacifism. I and many other teenagers were greatly influenced by his views. He was a good and sincere man, who finished his days in the parish of Bosham, near Chichester Harbour.

Outstanding events of those years included outings to the Devil's Dyke by steam railway, or by char-a-banc to Hassocks or Burgess

Hill Pleasure Gardens.

Our trip to the Devil's Dyke started from Brighton station. We were packed like sardines into wooden carriages and soon began the slow journey via Holland Road and Aldrington Halts, before starting the heavy pull up the steep gradient to the Dyke Station, with views of the sea and the Downs all around us. At times the engine pulled so slowly that people could walk alongside at a steady pace and keep up with the train. A friend has told me of one Good Friday trip when the guard leapt out, after instructing the children not to touch the lever, picked a bunch of wild flowers to distribute, and leapt on again.

The station nestled in a slight hollow where farm buildings now stand. It seemed a long trek walking in a crocodile from there to the summit of the Dyke HIll. I have no memory of how we amused ourselves all day. The Edwardian fun fairs, cableway and steep-grade funicular railway on the north slope of the Dyke Hill, which my Dad used to recall so vividly, had all disappeared long ago, leaving only a small concrete base and a tangled cable-wire to mark their former site. My Dad once told us that when he was a young man, in the year of the opening of the funicular railway in 1897, he was pushed from the top of the north slope and slid to the bottom. His best suit never looked the same again. I think of that still, and laugh to myself, when I walk past the remains of the concrete base.

To return to our Dyke outing, my clearest memory is connected with the journey home, when above the noise of the steaming engine and the rattle of the wheels, we raised our voices and sang:

> "We're on our journey home,
> God bless the engineman
> For bringing us safely home".

That marked the culmination of a day of mixed pleasures, but home was where I really liked to be.

When we took our outing to Hassocks Pleasure Garden it seemed a tremendous trip to a foreign land. My Mum with her lively enjoyment could persuade me onto the swings, but never onto the plank-swing, overloaded with sitting places, while the two end-standers grasping the metal supports worked it up to a fair swinging pace. There were bicycles you could ride round a track for a penny, and a single-track miniature railway-trolley which ran down an incline and had to be pushed up again for a second go.

These memories merge with those of Burgess Hill Garden, so I cannot remember which place sported a barrel-organ jangling out its plaintive tunes, while we stamped our feet, sheltering from the rain, and waiting for the hot tea from the enamel jug.

So the sun did not always shine, and there were times when I secretly thought these communal jaunts were highly overrrated, but always responded to the usual question "Well, have you enjoyed yourself?" with a polite "Yes thank you".

Chapter IV

SCHOOL AND AFTER

As I said at the end of Chapter One, education took off for me at the age of seven, and coincided with my move from Coombe Road Infants School to the temporary school housed in Moulsecoomb Place. Graciously proportioned rooms were filled with desks and blackboards. There were shrubberies and flower beds around the old house, and a pond, into which some boy inevitably fell in icy weather. Miss Knight and our neighbour Miss Nicholls taught in rooms at the front of the house. The back of the house was timbered with small windows, and a visit to Mr Vic Taylor's room along a dark passage was a "scarey" experience. I remember being sent on an errand to him, and unexpectedly coming upon my own image in a large mirror in a dim corridor.

We were taught local history, and told how the former owner of Moulsecoomb Place had received regular visits from the Prince Regent who later became George IV. Nature walks were a regular part of the timetable, and names of trees and their fruits were easy to remember when the beechnuts and conkers lay around our feet, to be freely gathered. Games and Competitive Sports were very popular and took place on a field adjoining Preston Barracks. We children took ourselves to school, crossing the main Lewes to Brighton road without great danger. The mail coach, heading for Lewes with its post-horn blower sitting aloft, was regularly to be seen then, but buses to take us into town were non-existent. Even then, the main road claimed its victims, and I can still remember a school mate in white shirt, shorts and socks running across the road on Sports Day, but never reaching the far side alive, to take part in his race.

When Miss Nicholls was my teacher, she organised a collection of food at harvest time, to be given to a local hospital. I asked my Mum for something just as I was dashing off to school, and she pushed a 2lb jar of blackberry jam wrapped in a blue sugar bag into my arms with firm instructions not to drop it. Of course the inevitable happened, and I presented the sticky mess to my beloved teacher to let her see that I had not forgotten her words. I can still see the look of distaste on her face as she said, "That belongs in the waste paper basket, don't you think?" I never told my Mum about the accident. When she said, "Well, did you get it there?" and I replied in the affirmative, I said to myself "Well, I did get it there, didn't I?"

Before I was ten, I had moved into the new Moulsecoomb Junior School, a bungalow-type building with a covered glass verandah and folding windows to every classroom. Beyond the playground and ornamental fruit trees, cows grazed in a field which in summer was yellow with buttercups. The mooing of the cows as they trod in monotonous file at milking times, proved a pleasant diversion from lessons, especially when the windows were folded back. I remember one such occasion when I was in Mr Taylor's class. He taught our class admirably, despite the diversions of the external world, with the help of a well-aimed piece of chalk or blackboard cloth. But this time he used a new tactic. Having failed to gain our attention over a problem on the blackboard, he suddenly switched course and said in a friendly manner, "Do you know what the inside of a cow's stomach is like? It goes round and round and round", suiting the action to the words. He soon had all eyes on him then, and with a quiet word of thanks he continued his problem.

Miss Knight was my first teacher in the new school. Miss Knight taught us sewing and knitting, but when it came to my knitting she passed me by, saying that she couldn't teach anyone knitting who was left handed. I went home and threw myself in the armchair, completely miserable. "What's the matter with you?" enquired my Mum with her back to me, on her knees and polishing the kitchen range. When I told her, she was quite indignant and incredulous. "Not teach you to knit? Come here!" she said, and rubbing her dirty hands on her apron, in a trice she produced wool and needles, sat in the armchair with me with her arms round mine and her hands over mine, and soon I could knit." Good old Mum", I thought. My other memory of Miss Knight is that she kept a large sweet jar on the shelf in her cupboard. If you did something well, you got a reward. I stood in front of the class and recited "The

Jan of Windmill Land - A Moulsecoomb School production, 1929. Ruby is in the back row, far right.

Brook" by Tennyson, the refrain of which goes:

"I chatter chatter as I go
To join the brimming river,
For men may come and men may go
But I go on for ever".

I certainly went on for ever, as I knew it right through. My reward was to push my hand down into the big sweet jar and retrieve one sticky pink satin-cushion.

Mr Taylor, my second teacher, gave us musical appreciation lessons. We sat on the hall floor while listening to classical records on his wind-up gramophone. Sometimes the music went out of tune if he did not rewind in time. But he played us the Rakoczy March by Berlioz and Schubert's Unfinished Symphony, and I shall always remember him for that. He also took us on historical outings. I can remember one occasion when we were taken to the Elizabethan mansion, Wiston House near Storrington, and were told that it was built in the shape of an E, and that it had previously been the home of the Shirley family. As it is no longer open to the public I should count myself fortunate.

School Pantomimes became a regular event in the new school and I had a secret longing to be the Good Fairy in "The Sleeping Beauty". But my sturdy build and dark complexion landed me the part of the Wicked Witch and with that I had to be content. I have

Ruby, aged nine, was among the first batch of entrants to the new Moulsecoomb Junior School in 1930

Ruby and her friend Kathleen setting out on their first day as scholarship girls at Varndean Grammar School a class photograph, taken when I was in Mr Taylor's class and there were forty five of us. Yet we were well taught, I am sure, and a few of us who were too young, had to be kept back another year before we could take our Scholarship Examination. How did the teachers manage such large classes? I think the children of my year were very fortunate, because each teacher we had, later left to become a Head Teacher.

The problem of large classes must have been slightly relieved with the opening of Moulsecoomb Secondary Schools. A group of us who were "marking time" before being allowed to take the eleven plus exam, joined a class of younger children and were housed for a year in the new Secondary Girls' School. Miss Moore was our kind teacher who taught English and Music, both of which I enjoyed. We had to get used to being taught by various teachers for different subjects and also moving from room to room. It was a good initiation for our move to secondary school where we settled in more easily when the time came.

In 1932 I passed the eleven-plus exam which was the passport to a Grammar School education.

The year I started going to Varndean Girls School marked the start of marginally less worrying times financially for my parents. Irene, the eldest girl was now teaching and living away from home. Kathleen, the second sister, was working in Brighton and contributing towards the family finances, while I had been successful in gaining a Hedgecock Scholarship which brought with it certain financial rewards. My Mum considered us well-off enough now to pay a tailoress to make my navy school coat. My kind sister, Kathleen, made the tunics and blouses to save money. She also made clothes for herself and the rest of the family. She was always generous, and when, as a young apprentice she came home with her first week's pay of three half crowns, from Colbournes, (the high-class furnishing store in Western Road), she held them in her hand in delight and said to me "Look, now I can buy your chocolate every day!"

My chief pal during those years was Kathleen who lived in The Highway. I was always lazy and late in the mornings so she used to come and knock on the door and entertain me during our long walk to the top of Ditchling Road with accounts of last night's radio play, or her doings at the Girls' Brigade in Lewes Road. She was more athletic than me, and I considered that she had a much more exciting life. On the way home we took a long detour through Stanmer Park Villas, via the beechwoods. We had great fun tree climbing and daring each other to do jumps. We met boys from Varndean Boys' School who chased us and left rude messages on walls. We balanced on tops of garden walls in Stanmer Villas or Roedale Road, until window-taps from irate residents sent us scurrying off. We often had the sense to stuff our hats in our satchels so that we could not be identified.

When we got to the Swing Park at the bottom of Hollingdean Road we played there a long time. The high slide was on sloping ground and very dangerous. If you could land on two feet when you shot off the end of it, you were lucky. I never was, being fat! I asked my Mum if she minded my late return home. She said it was good to play before having to get down to my homework, as long as I got home before Dad. Once, sitting on the top of the slide, I saw his familiar high-crowned trilby hat passing along the top of the wall. I shot down the slide in fear, grazing my back on the dirt and gravel, and ran home the back way via Southall Avenue, arriving just before Dad to the amusement of my Mum.

Those seven years of hard work and play at Varndean were good years to look back on. Learning came easily to me and for the first five years I was nearly always top of my class in exams, partly because I was encouraged to work so hard at my homework by my family, but also because I had a good memory and could learn off strings of notes and facts. I crammed my head with knowledge and then promptly forgot it as soon as exams were over. I was not brilliant at any subject, just a "good all-rounder" and I have never been an intellectual.

During my Dad's severe illness and consequent death, while I was in the Sixth Form, my work seemed to suffer and I knew that my dreams of going to University would never come to pass. Many of my former school friends were now out to work and I began to feel that I should be doing the same. I began to hanker after pretty clothes and smart shoes, but knew that my parents had decided I was to be a teacher like sister Irene, and I did not want to let them down. However, there were many compensations and I enjoyed the experience of singing in the choir and taking part in team games. I had tennis lessons, played in the hockey team and took part in school plays.

I do not remember that we scholarship girls were treated in any way differently from the fee-paying girls. It was sometimes noticeable that uniforms looked "scruffy" on some girls, but my Mum and sisters would never allow that to happen. I felt that I was as smart as the next girl, even though my garments were handmade at home. Hockey sticks and tennis racquets could be borrowed if you could not afford to buy your own. Miss Ellis the Headmistress, and Miss Strange the Deputy, both Graduates of Cambridge and Oxford, I gazed on with a mixture of respect and fear, but they treated all their girls the same. The only member of staff who upset us was a younger Maths teacher who used to call out individual girls to her desk when their homework was bad or missing, and remark: "I really can't think what sort of homes some of you girls come from".

My friendships widened and my pal through school and college became Tib, short for Dorothy Tibbalds, who was also a scholarship girl. She came from an interesting Brighton family who lived near St Nicholas Church in Dyke Road. Her Uncle Bert was a violin maker and repairer, and his lounge was hung with musical instruments. Her Dad played the violin, her sister the piano, and she herself played the cello. I remember some happy musical evenings, and some equally happy ones playing poker with the family in their basement room. Tib was later to marry a Canadian soldier from Ontario whom she met at the Regent Dance Hall. We still corresponded and have met on rare ocasions. She has a daughter and two grandsons.

At school we had a mutual friend called Norah, one of the fee-paying girls who lived in a Regency house in Crown Street. She had rosy cheeks and blue eyes with a roguish expression. She formed a secret society among her friends, and our initiation ceremonies behind the bicycle shed included being pricked with a pin to draw blood. She appeared to be somewhat defiant of authority, and told us she had been moved to Varndean from the High School, in the hope that she would emulate the scholarship girls and work harder. She finally did brilliantly and obtained a place at Cambridge; then later, after her graduation, married a lecturer and brought up her family in Jamaica.

Sometimes I wonder to myself whatever happened to those other Moulsecoomb girls I knew who won their scholarships to Varndean Grammar School. I have kept up with only two of them, who became my friends throughout our lives. Dorothy joined the WAAF at the outbreak of war and later married a Flight Officer. They have three sons, one of whom is an accountant, the second a solicitor and the third has a position in the Bank of England. Rita joined the WRNS and later married a naval officer. They had a daughter and a son. Their daughter lives in New York, is married to a prominent American writer and film producer, and is a novelist herself. Their son married into a family of University academics and lives in the Home Counties. On her husband's retirement Rita lived with him in the Cathedral Close at Salisbury until their recent deaths within three years of each other.

In my mid-teens I deserted my church at Moulsecoomb, and began to attend St Nicholas Church, where I joined the Guides with Tib and was confirmed. We had weekend country walks together and shared camping and seaside holidays. Later we both managed to gain places at Goldsmiths' College, London. Our college was one of the first targets of the German firebombs in the Autumn of 1939. So our college finished up in Nottingham, sharing the premises of the University. The choice of Goldsmiths had been suggested by our new Head, Miss Warmington. It was one of the few places where you could sit for a General Degree without attending a University. It was also one of the first "mixed" male and female Teacher training colleges in the country.

I planned initially to take a three-year course with English as my main subject. I had first to resit my Latin Inter Arts before Christmas. The confusion of the late start to the term in Nottingham together with a shortage of lecturers made this impractical, so instead I took the normal Teacher's Course with Tib.

The years in Nottingham proved a maturing experience. I met

Schoolfriends

Kathleen, Norah and Tib (top to bottom), all sixteen, pictured in 1937 at Varndean.

"We did not know this was being taken", wrote Ruby on the back of this photo, taken at Nottingham in 1940. Tib and Mary share the picnic.

young people from every part of Britain and from overseas. I liked many of them and learned to appreciate their differences. I was unprepared for the clannishness of the Welsh contingent at our college, but could forgive them their apparently unfriendly ways when, gathered together in one corner of the crowded refectory, they would suddenly burst into spontaneous part-singing. I was unprepared for the snobbishness of a Nottingham factory-owner, who considered that a "London student" was not good enough for his son to be associating with.

I heard first-hand what it was like to work in Players Cigarette Factory, and began to realise that the free daily pint of milk and high wages were a cover up for the fact that many employees finished up with cancer. I went down a coalmine and had a two hour conducted tour underground, crawling along in places; realising on my return to upper air that no wages could be high enough to pay a man who spent his life down there. I experienced the Nottingham Palais de Danse and the Music Hall. I recognised civic pride in the City of Nottingham and realised that they spent far more on their schools and education than we in the opulent South. I learned to teach and try to understand the accents of the local children. I also learned to row on University College Lake and on the River Trent, and danced to the strains of the College Band whose signature tune was "In the Mood".

The dangers of war touched us very lightly in comparison with London and the South Coast. I remember the choking smoke-screen which was sent up after dark every evening to shield the city; and the night that Coventry was attacked and burnt, we stood and watched the glow from the roof of the University Library where we were firewatching. Apart from doing minor civilian duties and becoming blood donors during the height of the bombing, we did not contribute greatly to the war effort, unless our infectious high-spirits contributed something to the country's morale. Mary, a college friend, lived at Sleaford in Lincolnshire, and on some weekends invited me to share in the social life of the officer's mess at Cranwell.

By contrast, my holidays from college spent in Brighton were much more grim. As my Dad had died before I left school, Mum was having a struggle to keep me at college and the strain of the war as well was affecting her health. We used to spend long night-hours in the cupboard under the stairs when the bombing got bad. Food was always short, in comparison with the good college fare. I had to obtain Emergency Ration Cards from the Food Office whenever I came back home on holiday, but all the extra food it gave my Mum to deal with was as follows:

Butter	2 oz	Bacon	3 oz
Lard	1 oz	Sugar	half pound
Margarine	4 oz	Meat	1s 2d worth
Cheese	2 oz	Fresh milk	2 pints
Fresh eggs	1		

Ruby at nineteen
(1940)

Peter at twenty-four
(1943)

Brighton and the coast became a prohibited area. One had to carry a special pass if travelling in and out. The buses stopped early in the evenings, and with all the blackout restrictions there was little one could do in the way of entertainment. As I had met a Brighton boy whom I was very fond of, while I was still at school, and still saw him from time to time though he was in the Army, I spent my days and evenings making and embroidering things for my "bottom drawer", in the hopes that we could have a home together when Hitler had finished with us.

Peter Dunn had been Deputy Head Boy at Varndean Grammar School for Boys. I told Mum that he knew my cousin Bernard at School, so that was a good start. I met him while queuing for the Gallery at the Theatre Royal where Tib and I used to go on a Saturday when we could afford it. The only way I managed it was by walking to School every day and saving my bus fare. We were mad on the theatre and worshipped Diana Wynyard and Isobel Jeans, Ivor Novello and Noel Coward, and many more with illustrious names. One week Tib didn't turn up, and this man I had noticed previously in the Gallery walked up to me in the queue and said: "Excuse me, but are you the beginning or the end?"

When I was first "taken out" (because he was working in a Bank in London at that time), I was offered China tea and toast in Lyons at the corner of St James Street. I thought this the height of sophistication. On a later meeting, fish and chips out of newspaper, purchased in Edward Street, was suggested and he seemed relieved when I accepted it. His next question was: "What newspaper do you read?" When I told him we took the *Daily Herald* I felt I had his approval. I took him home to meet Mum and he liked her and her cheese scones, and she liked him. We sympathised with each other because both of us had widowed mothers. Peter's mother had been a widow since the early 1920s, as a result of her husband's bad health after the First World War, and she ran an apartment house in Kemptown.

We both had pacifist views for religious reasons and Peter was also a member of the Peace Pledge Union. I told him about my Uncle Dick, although he never met him until years later, after the war. Peter had been before a Tribunal, and was granted exemption from military service. However, later wartime events made him change his attitude and he volunteered for the Army before he was 22, and spent some time living under canvas in the snow, with little equipment. He suffered ill health for much of the war, after that disastrous start.

Chapter V

FULL CIRCLE

The only way Mum managed to send me to college when she was left a widow, was by begging the British Legion to help the daughter of an ex-soldier. They kindly gave me a small grant. Then Brighton Education Committee offered me a substantial loan on the understanding that the money was repaid within the first two years of teaching, by a deduction from the monthly salary cheque. This meant that for financial reasons I was forced to return to Brighton to teach, even though I had been interviewed and accepted by Edmonton Education Committee. I knew that my Mum needed my financial help at home, but part of me felt resentful that I could not become a London teacher with the status, in those days, of the highest salary scale.

In September 1941 I started my first teaching job at Whitehawk. I found it tough going, but my Head Teacher, Miss Brooker, was one of the best I ever had. She was also the President of the Brighton N.U.T. She was a strong healthy-looking woman, a keen swimmer, with a bluff hearty manner, who could stand up well to the threats and verbal attacks of parents. If a local Mum rushed into the school with a grievance, rolling up her sleeves in anticipation of a bit of a barney, I have seen my Head roll up her sleeves and face her, which usually had the effect of ensuring a reasonable discussion. I felt sympathy for those parents and their children, however difficult their behaviour, because in the isolated Downland estate, they were only suffering the same traumas as my own neighbours in North and East Moulsecoomb.

At the end of my first year of teaching, I married Peter when he came home on leave.

Ever practical, it seemed pointless to me to wait till after the war to wed, when we could be saving my Serviceman's Wife's Allowance in the Post Office, to form a little nest-egg for our future home.

I was recovering from an attack of jaundice at the time, so my yellow skin rather clashed with the colour of my crushed-strawberry crepe dress, which I had made myself and which now hung loosely on my thin frame. Our wedding cake was minute, but was the result of months of self denial on the part of my family. It was hidden under a great cardboard show-case and had no icing or decorations to crown it. We bought a few bottles and just asked a few relatives and friends round to Mum's house after the ceremony at St Andrew's, Moulsecoomb. The service was conducted by my friend and helper the Reverend Bransby Jones. I shall never forget his kindness during my Dad's illness, nor his concern when I was ill prior to my wedding.

Are you the beginning or the end? By West Pier in 1941 with husband-to-be Peter, on leave from the army

From this day forward... 12 August 1942, outside St Andrews, Moulsecoomb. With the newly-weds are (front row, L to R) Kathleen, Ruby's Mum, Tib and Irene. Peter's Mum is at the back, far right

We spent an evening at the cinema and then Peter returned to his base in Lincolnshire. He was a gentle intellectual, with a strong aversion to killing his fellow men. His health problems kept him within the British Isles and he was engaged in non-combatant duties, so we could see each other regularly.

My second year of teaching seemed to coincide with the Germans' second attack on London and the South Coast. Whitehawk School was damaged by machine gunning. Pellets broke the windows and came to rest in the desk lids, luckily, before the children had arrived. I had just completed a night of firewatching duty on the school premises, and diminutive Mr Darling had just arrived for his Caretaker duties, when there was an almighty row overhead. The next moment I found myself (all five foot eight inches of me!) pinned against the corridor wall with the little Caretaker's arms around my waist. He was saying, "It's alright, I'll take care of you." I just refrained from saying, "Thank you, Darling."

It was a wearying period, with disturbed nights, and almost as much time spent in the school shelters as the classrooms. Teaching was severely disrupted but we tried chanting tables, or learning poetry, and when these failed, singing popular songs. Brighton had its share of bombing and machine-gun attacks. The Odeon Cinema in Paston Place, the School Clinic in Circus Street, the Railway Viaduct in Preston Road all came under attack and lives were lost. Many small homes were lost as well.

Despite the anti aircraft barrage, individual enemy planes used to come in low over the cliffs at Black Rock, before the air raid warning sounded on some occasions. St Mark's School was an easy target, and once, while waiting for a bus outside the chemist's shop opposite the school, a bomb landed in the playground. The chemist dragged me in to crouch under his counter seconds before the explosion. One teacher was killed, another was blown from the top to the bottom of the building.

The saddest day of that year for me, was the day I was asked by Miss Brooker to do her a favour while she took my class. She had left some swimming certificates in her flat which she needed that day. Travelling back from Hove on the bus, I heard the air raid warning but continued my journey to Arundel Road and began walking up Whitehawk Valley. Suddenly I was aware of an enemy plane flying so low over the houses that I could clearly see the pilot and gunner. I dashed into a garden and stood flat against the house wall. When the plane had passed over I saw pellets on the ground and pock-marks in the concrete wall. A woman came out and said "Thank God you're safe. I thought they had got you." I walked on to school to meet a very agitated Headmistress striding up and down the playground while the staff and children were in the shelters. She looked unwell, but relieved to see me. She said she was glad to see me back safely and thanked me, and that was the last time I ever spoke to her, because she died that same night from a burst appendix.

Mr A.E. Kitchen, who retired in 1955, was Ruby's Head at Moulsecoomb Junior School when she was there both as child and teacher. He was also Chairman of the Moulsecoomb Ratepayers Association.

There was a delay of many months before the appointment of a new Head Teacher. Had I known it was to be my old friend Mr Vic Taylor, I may well have have stayed at Whitehawk. As it was, I decided to transfer to Moulsecoomb and went to another old friend, Mr Kitchen, and began teaching there in the Autumn of 1944. So there I was, back to the school of my childhood, but not for long. No sooner had my appointment been confirmed than I was told that it would be my turn, as the newest member of staff, to go to Yorkshire in November, and look after the small number of evacuees from Moulsecoomb, who were still living up there. In November 1944 my Mum, as Welfare Officer, and myself as teacher, set off by train for the mining villages of Wales and Kiveton near Sheffield.

Those six months in Yorkshire were a life-saver for my Mum. We were billetted with Mrs Gates, wife of a local teacher serving in Italy, and herself a trained cook. Food was not short in the rural districts of the North. What is more, we enjoyed months of uninterrupted sleep at night. Despite the snow and bitter cold, Mum enjoyed the responsibility of visiting the various miner's wives with whom the Brighton evacuees were living. The walking kept her fit, and there was always a welcome by a warm fire, and a cup of tea at the end of it. Some evenings we worked with the Red Cross voluntary workers giving out used clothing and shoes to the children. On Saturdays we took a shopping bus into Sheffield, sat in cafes and ate unrationed food, then queued under the pall of the stinking smoke-screen, for a crowded noisy bus back.

It was like entering a new world for my Mum to be among those friendly Notherners. For myself it was a question of endurance until the Spring. I loved the children who were so well disciplined and polite; it was like a breath from a past age; but I had to teach in half a classroom, raising my voice above that of my fellow-teacher. We tried to organise our oral lessons in relays, but it was not easy. The building was Victorian and had never been modernised. The Head, who was awaiting retirement, appeared to match the building and could be seen, once a day only, marching in the passageway wielding a cane. Parents never entered the building and appeared to live by the philosophy that teachers know best. I can still visualise one sturdy nine year old miner's son, standing in his black boots and reciting "Dobbin" by Alfred Noyes:

> "Owd 'orse Dobbin owt at grass
> Turns 'is tail to t'winds 'at pass",

he declaimed in his broad accent and didn't stop until the end.

As for the few Moulsecoomb children living in the mining village, they were now unrecognisable as Southerners. They had been taken with care and concern into miner's families. Some of them never had a letter or a present from home, and at the end of the war were adopted by their foster parents.

Mum and I returned home gladly, to meet the full force of the "doodlebugs" over Brighton and the South. Our days and nights were now disturbed by an overhead din like noisy old motorbikes, followed by an eerie silence before the bomb found its target. Despite this, I was happy to be teaching in my old school, and to have the anticipation of teaching my own class for a full year. Mr Kitchen was, no doubt, having discipline problems, with a practically all-female staff who were coping with large classes.

But I was certain that I would find my work more enjoyable than at Whitehawk. I would make the most of the school's rural setting and develop the children's interest in nature. This elation was short-lived when I was confronted with one empty cupboard, and a few moth-eaten piles of text books in the other. I made do with rough paper in place of exercise books, and sheets of old newspaper for artwork, until one memorable day when I was called into the empty classroom of Miss Hemsworth, one of the elderly members of staff. She must have liked me for some reason, because, shaking her bunch of keys like a chatelaine, she unlocked and revealed a cupboard full of pre-war stock from top to bottom. My eyes opened wide to see top quality art and pastel paper, crayons, paints, squirrel-hair brushes, and exercise books. "Where did this come from?" I asked as she loaded my arms with gold dust. "Ah", she replied with a smile and a wink. "It's no good getting old if you don't get artful." That phrase has now become a household saying.

This was the year I met Jimmy with his big brown eyes and mop of black hair. Attempting to teach him to read was the most frustrating task of my young career, not encouraged by the fact that Jimmy's Mum came to see me to tell me that if teaching to read caused all this upset, she would rather the lad did not learn to read at all. After all, his Dad couldn't read, and he was getting along alright. I discovered later, that he belonged to a family of gypsies who had been housed at East Moulsecoomb for the war period in order to qualify for civilian ration cards.

This was also the year of the memorable note brought to me by Billy's little brother, written by Mum on a scrap of blue sugar paper and stating -"Billy can't come to school as his face has come out through his stomach." Miss Piercy, I think it was, who capped my note with a better one which said "Johnny can't come because he hasn't been. I've given him something to make him go, and when he's been he'll come." But I only have her word for it, and saw no written proof!

The following year at school was memorable for two reasons. The celebration of V.E. Day meant that hostilities would soon be at an end. Secondly, the first "demobbed" Servicemen came back to their teaching posts. Reg from the R.A.F. and Maurice from the R.N. were two I remember. Maurice kept a low profile and enjoyed the boys' cricket. Reg made his mark by stating that what this school needed was a bit of discipline. He walked about the room with a leather tawse which he placed on his desk in front of the class. I only learnt this from my monitor, who went on messages and returned in chastened mood. "How does he think we women have been coping, all through the war years?" I asked myself indignantly. When I heard him ranting in our cloakroom, I felt almost as scared as my well-behaved Class 3A, and also very sad. Was this the way things were to go?

As it happened, I did not have many months to discover. My husband was discharged from the Army in February 1946, with rheumatic and heart troubles. He obtained temporary work in the Food Office, while thinking about his future career. He had no desire to return to his pre-war job in Cook's Bank, Berkeley Street, since he could not afford to commute to London and keep a wife on the salary offered. My earnings would not last much longer, as I was pregnant. However, I was glad to learn that, for the first time in their history, women teachers were being encouraged to return to their posts after having a baby. I was the first woman teacher at Moulsecoomb to be offered that option, and I decided to take advantage of it, with my Mum's support.

Meanwhile, Peter hovered around my classroom occasionally, watching me teach, and finally announced that he wanted to go to Eastbourne Emergency College to train as a teacher. Mr Kitchen, my Headmaster, was an old soldier who had been awarded the M.M. in the First World War. He was also a keen member of the British Legion. He chatted with Peter who had been registered as disabled, and advised me that he should apply for an Army

With Christina, 3 months, in 1947. Taken in the garden at Preston Road.

In this Moulsecoomb staff photo Ruby is in the back row, with the demobbed Reg and Maurice to her left. Mr Kitchen is fourth left in the middle row.

disablement pension. Peter also procured a small Government Student Grant, so things would be tight but we would manage somehow. Since Peter's demobilisation we had been living in rooms in Preston Road, above a Nursery School run by an acquaintance and fellow student from Goldsmith's College. There I lived, for most of the time alone, with our baby daughter Christina Mary. The week she was born had coincided with Peter's first week at college. He was a boarder but came home every weekend.

By the late Spring of 1947, when Christina was barely four months old, I was back teaching again at Moulsecoomb. I was up at 6 a.m. tending the baby and going off with her, and supplies for the day, to Mum's at Moulsecoomb. My life seemed to have come full circle. I had to take two buses, changing at St Peter's Church. After settling Christina in with Mum, I walked to the school and started my real job. By then school canteens had been established, and there was a long dinner hour, so I was able to have a meal before walking back to Mum's to feed and play with baby for a while before the afternoon session began.

Teaching conditions had deteriorated since the war. The over-crowding that year was so great that the School Hall had been made into two classrooms with a small portable screen between. Guess who had one of those classrooms? It was a condition to be endured rather than enjoyed, and I was not sorry when Peter's course ended, and he started teaching in Brighton, in March 1948.

Dorothy Stringer, Mayor of Brighton in 1952-53, was made freeman of the Borough of Brighton in 1968, at which time she was in her mid-seventies and served on forty committees. She was Chairman of Brighton Education Committee, of which she was a member for fifty years. Dorothy Stringer School, opened in 1955, was named after her.

I then settled back into domesticity very happily for a few years. Mum was the loser because she missed caring for her little granddaughter. So I still made regular visits to Moulsecoomb two or three times a week, and kept in touch with staff from the school, even after the birth of my second daughter Julia in 1950, until the retirement of Mr Kitchen a few years later.

In 1954 I started as a supply teacher, taking my little daughter with me for the first year. I moved around from Carden School to Patcham, St Lukes, Fairlight, Central, St Pauls and Stanford. Peter was meanwhile teaching at St Johns, St Lukes and Middle Street. He kept to town schools so that he could keep an eye on his aged widowed mother every day. After her death he concentrated on his main interest which was the study of emotional disturbance in children. He took a Diploma Course at London University, and from there moved to West Sussex, to be in charge of a Day Unit.

In 1961, as soon as Christina and Julia had both obtained places at Grammar Schools, I applied for full-time employment because I needed to supplement the family income and have the security of a permanent post with the Authority. Before my application had been confirmed, I was surprised one morning by an unannounced visitor to my classroom. In one quick glance my eye took in the handsome hat and the beads hanging on an ample bosom. Here in the flesh was the local celebrity I had so often seen portrayed in newspaper photographs in her capacity as Chairman

When Mum moved away from The Avenue, we never wanted to visit Moulsecoomb again

This picture of Ruby's mother in her beloved garden at the old house was taken around 1970, when Mrs Pennifold was in her eighties of Brighton Education Committee. She was also, I had been told, on the Management Committee of the school where I was then doing supply teaching, Stanford School. Before she could announce herself I turned to the class and said: "Stand up children, we have a very important visitor this morning to see you - Miss Dorothy Stringer". They stood and chanted "Good morning" and we shook hands.

It seemed to go down well, for I shortly received notification that my application for full-time teaching had been granted, and soon after that I moved to Patcham Junior and Middle School.

When Mum moved away from The Avenue in the early seventies, to live in a flat bought by my sister Irene in Florence Road, we never wanted to visit Moulsecoomb again. Mum was very upset at leaving her old home after fifty years, but a much needed modernisation scheme was in progress and tenants were being temporarily moved out. She was by this time in her 80s, and severely disabled as well as partially sighted, so it was better for her to be in a convenient ground floor flat with Irene. We have never been back to see the old home again. We are told that we would not recognise it, so it is best remembered as it was.

We did not however abandon all interest in the estate, for little snippets of news came through to us from former neighbours. News of Moulsecoomb School came from two Church friends, one of whom was a School Secretary, and the other a Deputy

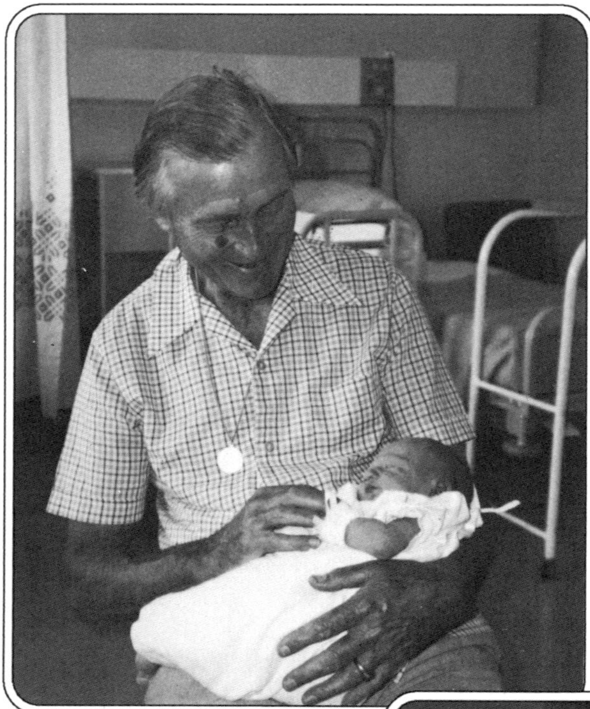

Doting grandparents

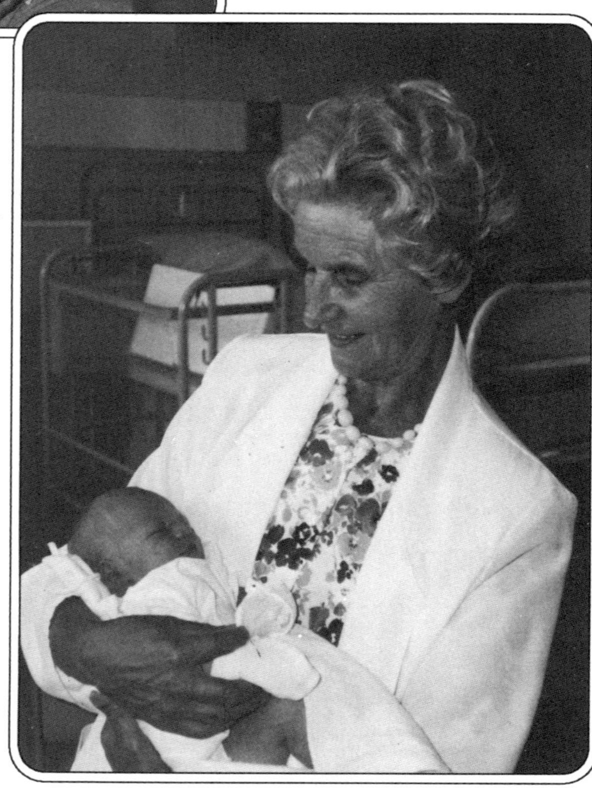

Peter and Ruby with daughter Julia's son Jack Peter, in 1989

Head. Their store of anecdotes seemed endless, also sad stories of continual vandalism. I was told that there was a Corporation glazier on duty most of the time repairing the damage. Teaching was hard, rewards were few and with problems of unemployment increasing, the estate was designated an Educational Priority Area. What a far cry from the idyllic Garden Suburb of the 1920s!

My dear old Mum died in 1978 in her ninety-third year. By then, with the ever-increasing demands of family life and the necessity for me to supplement the family income, my interest in Moulsecoomb had waned, and my support was now for the schools where my girls were, or the one where I was teaching. I leave it to someone else to continue the history of Moulsecoomb to the present day.

***

I taught at Patcham for nearly twenty years until retirement. Peter retired ten months after me, following major heart surgery. We both keep busy still. Peter pursues his forty-year interest in poetry writing and publication and keeps up a varied correspondence with friends. I write prose in minor ways varying from personal letters to a prizewinning magazine letter, an article in a local schools publication and a handwritten book for my grandchildren about their great-grandmother.

We see our girls and their families frequently and enjoy watching the growth of the young ones. We still share our love of the countryside, and delight in the privilege of making our visits at quiet times, when most of the world is at work. It sometimes crosses our minds that we might move from Sussex, but I doubt if we ever will.

THE END

About this book

This book was made by Nick Osmond, Andy Fisher, Georgina Attrell and Jackie Connatty, with Ruby Dunn.

Thanks to Peter Dickens, Brighton Plans Registry, Brighton Reference Library, East Sussex Record Office, Peggy Eaton, Terry Etherton, Peter Gilbert, Fred Gray, Mr Jeeves of Branch Two, Lavender Jones, Jane Kerr, John Patience and John Roles for kindly providing advice, photos, documents and maps, and to South East Arts for their financial support.

Special thanks to Mike Hayler, Carmel Kelly, Selma Montford, Peter Dunn, Al Thomson and the QueenSpark manuscripts group.

Very special thanks to Lynn Rogers who designed the cover at short notice.

Published in May 1990 by QueenSpark Books, Lewis Cohen Urban Studies Centre, 68 Grand Parade, Brighton BN2 2JY.

Printed by Faulwood & Herbert, Preston Village, Brighton.

 ISBN 0 904735 1

About QueenSpark

QueenSpark is a community writing and publishing group based in Brighton. We believe that anyone who wants to can be a writer and our aim is to encourage and publish writing by people who do not normally get into print. QueenSpark is not a commercial company. We have some part-time paid workers, but most of us are volunteers who work together to write and produce books, gaining and sharing skills and confidence as we go.

We have a number of active writing workshops in Brighton and Hove, women only and mixed. Our manuscripts group reads all manuscripts, decides which ones to publish and sets up a book-making group. All groups are run on a co-operative basis and are free. Membership of QueenSpark is £2 waged or £1 unwaged. If you would like to get involved, ring us on Brighton 571916, or write to QueenSpark Books, Lewis Cohen Urban Studies Centre, 68 Grand Parade, Brighton BN2 2JY.

QueenSpark is a member of the national Federation of Worker Writers and Community Publishers. If you live outside Brighton we can give you the address of your nearest Federation group. QueenSpark gratefully acknowledges funding from South East Arts, Brighton Borough Council, Hove Borough Council and East Sussex County Council.

Other QueenSpark Books

Since the early 1970s we have published 24 books, mainly local autobiographies, but also books of humour, poetry, history and politics. Many of them have sold out one or more editions. Following is a list of the books which are currently in print:

1. Poverty: Hardship but Happiness - Those were the days, 1903-1917. Albert Paul (1974, 1975, 1981). The story of a Brighton working class boy's life early this century. Price 50p

7. Live and Learn - a life and struggle for progress. Les Moss (1979). One man's trade union and political activism in London and Brighton from the 1920's onward. Price 60p

8. Faded Rainbow - our married years. Daisy Noakes (1980). Beautifully describes the life of a young town wife and mother, from 1934, isolated in the country near Gatwick Airfield, and tells how she coped with her husband's terminal illness. Price 75p

9. Hard Times and Easy Terms. Bert Healey (1980). The entertaining story of a Brighton cockney and wide boy. Price 90p

10. The Landlord Cometh. Jack Cummins (1981). The story of a London labour activist and conscientious objector who goes off to the first world war! Price 60p

12. Hard Work and No Consideration - 51 years as a carpenter-joiner, 1917-1968. Albert Paul (1981). Describes his working life in Brighton and around England during the war. Price 70p

13. Who was Harry Cowley? QueenSpark (1984). The controversial biography of a Brighton chimney sweep and local legend, known as 'the Gov'nor'. Price £1.50p

14. Who Stood Idly By. Alf Johns (1984). Humorous & political poems and cartoons by a retired hospital porter. Price 80p

15. Paper on the Wind. QueenSpark Women Writers (1984). Poetry and prose from our Women Writers' group. Price £1.50p

16. Growing up in Ditchling. Doris Hall (1985). A beautifully illustrated account of girlhood in a Sussex rural village in the early part of this century. Price £1.95

17. The Other Side of the Counter. Marjorie Gardiner (1985). A rumbustious account of work in a Brighton hat shop between the wars. Price £1.95

18. The Circle of Life. Olive Masterson (1986). A woman's story of her life in Brighton this century. Price £1.95

19. One Camp Chair in the Living Room - a woman's life in Rottingdean. Margaret Ward (1988). Set in a Sussex seaside village, the story of a family torn apart. Price £1.95

21. Everything Seems Smaller - a Brighton Boyhood between the Wars. Sid Manville (1989). A vivid account of growing up in Bear Road, Brighton between the wars. Price £2.50

22. Backstreet Brighton: photographs and memories of the fifties and sixties. QueenSpark Books and the Lewis Cohen Urban Studies Centre (1989). A sequel to Backyard Brighton (1988).Street photos taken by Brighton Coucil as a record of houses which have since been demolished, with the recollections of people who used to live in them. Price £3.95

23. Moulsecoomb Days - Learning and Teaching on a Brighton Council Estate, 1922-47. Ruby Dunn (1990). Traces the embattled creation of community in a "garden suburb" without so much as a school or church. Price £2.50

Brighton on the Rocks - Monetarism and the Local State. QueenSpark Rates Group (1983). Interviews, photos, statistics. Effects of monetarism on Brighton people. Price £2.00

Reminiscence Pack. Photographs and slides of Brighton this century. May be borrowed free of charge by OAP and community groups. The slides cover themes such as childhood, leisure, housing, transport and WW2. Pack of 110 slides costs £50

Education Packs. Two illustrated education packs based on the books by Albert Paul (*Poverty: Hardship but Happiness*) and Doris Hall (*Growing up in Ditchling*). Fun approaches to introduce pupils from eight upwards to the ways children's lives have changed this century. Price £3.00

QueenSpark Books

You can order our books by post. Write to us at QueenSpark Books, 68 Grand Parade, Brighton BN2 2JY or phone us on Brighton 571916. Please add 60p for each book to cover postage and packing and make cheques payable to QueenSpark Books.

On weekdays our books can be bought from the Lewis Cohen Urban Studies office on the ground floor, 68 Grand Parade, Brighton. They are also on sale at local bookshops and from our stall in Brighton's Upper Gardner Street Market on sunny Saturday mornings. A free publications list is available on request.

Small Holdings
F.P.
Stone
Stone
Stone
Stones
484
500
400
300
Road
527
Golf Course
Post
Post
Co. Boro. By.
Hollingbury Castle (Camp)
Flint Implements & Early Iron Age Pottery found A.D. 1908
Allotment Gardens
Upper Roedale
Moulsecoomb Pit
Pavilion
Sports Ground
MOULSECOOMB WILD PARK
Human Remains found A.D. 1928.
128
B.M. 134·59
B.S.
Coldean Wood
B.M. 184·38
166
198
Cold Dean
Co. Boro. By.
Nursery
148
170
200
NORTH MOULSECOOMB
RAILWAY
B.M. 118·99
Schools
Hodshrove
B.R.
N